A Voice in the Wilderness, volume 8

Ashes in the Morning

Dalen Garris

This is a work of history. Historical individuals and places and events are mentioned.

Copyright © 2021 by Dalen Garris

Published by Revivalfire Ministries
Cover design by Kevin Haislip

ISBN 13: 978-1-7342213-9-8

All rights reserved.
No part of this book may be used or reproduced in any manner whatsoever, without written permission, except in the case of brief quotations embodied in critical articles and reviews, as provided by U.S. Copyright Law.

All Scripture is from the King James Version

For information, address
dale@revivalfire.org

First paperback printing August, 2021

Printed in the United States of America

Dedication

"And he will destroy in this mountain the face of the covering cast over all people, and the vail that is spread over all nations.

He will swallow up death in victory; and the Lord GOD will wipe away tears from off all faces; and the rebuke of his people shall he take away from off all the earth: for the LORD hath spoken it.

And it shall be said in that day, Lo, this is our God; we have waited for him, and he will save us: this is the LORD; we have waited for him, we will be glad and rejoice in his salvation."

Isaiah 25:7-9

Table of Contents

Dedication	3
Real Church	1
Ashes in the Morning	5
No Anointing	7
Four R's	9
Feelings	13
Another World	15
A Little Girl Named Hope	17
Hell	21
Noah's Seven Days	23
Finding God	25
Grasp of God	29
The Deal with Hell	31
Mercy	35
Humpty Dumpty	39
The Harvest is Past	43
Psalm 91	47
The Wharf	51
The Furnace Room	53
Snow	57
Curtain of Night	59
Wedding Feast	61
Royal Falcons	63
Best Sellers	65
Thermometer for the Church	69
Sound Speech	71
Sorcery	73

Folly of Fools	77
Leprosy in the House	81
Water in the Desert	83
Prophetic Spirits	85
Insanity	89
Substance	91
Talk is Cheap	95
Drinking from the Bottle	97
Coming to Jordan	99
Answering a Fool	101
Jehoshaphat	105
A Glimpse	107
Yawn	109
The Esther Church	111
Fat and Lazy	115
Turned Unto Fables	117
Talk, Talk, Talk	121
Sandbar	125
Ten Pieces of Silver	127
Learning How to Die	129
Tied to the Dock	131
Things I Don't Understand	133
A Pot of Oil	137
About the Author	139

Real Church

Picture yourself entering a church at 7:30 PM. You've come because a perfect stranger walked up to you and told you that you should come. It wasn't the persuasiveness of his argument but the look in his eyes that intrigued you. Something exciting was happening that you did not want to miss.

So here you are, standing at the entrance getting ready to walk inside and see if this is the same old thing that you find at every other church in town or is this something special.

Church is okay, but you have felt like you have been tethered to lifeless churchy traditions and the stifling structure of preacher vs. congregation. Their one-dimensional arrangement leaves you feeling flat and hungry for something more. Even the well-meaning "Jesus" smiles and handshaking feel as plastic as the little Jesus on their dashboards. You want something more, so you have rejected "Churchianity" as you know it, and now you are standing outside another church about to put God to the test one more time. Will this be more of the same? Or will the promise of an electrifying experience that you saw in the eyes of that kid who witnessed to you unfold and change your life tonight?

You walk in with a little bit of trepidation, not knowing what to expect, but things seem normal ... until everyone else starts to arrive. The place is packed, wall-to-wall, with every kind of personality you can imagine – from drug dealers to priests, whores to housewives, nerds to jocks. It all feels a little out of the ordinary, but then, "ordinary" is not why you came here.

Services start with some rousing Gospel songs, and as you stand clapping your hands to the music, you can feel an excitement begin to enter the room. It's not just the music – it's something else that filters in through the songs you're singing. Whatever it is, you are a bit disappointed when the song service is over, and the next part of the service begins.

A few personal testimonies, some quick announcements, a short offering – this isn't that different from the type of church services you have seen before, but somehow, it all feels completely new.

But when the preacher comes to the pulpit and begins to preach, you become aware of a feeling that seems to pervade this whole place. As he gets going, the cadence of the message begins to take on a roll of its own, and there is a resonance in the preacher's voice that echoes, not in your ears but in your heart. It's as if God Himself is rolling through this place, over the pulpit, and speaking right into your soul. You can feel the Spirit of God in this place like you have never felt it before in your life. As a matter of fact, you have <u>never</u> felt anything like this.

Services end with an altar call – not a "pity" line to pray for your ailments, weaknesses, and shortcomings, but to give your heart to Jesus Christ and ask God to save you. This isn't an ecclesiastical display of public confirmation but a supernatural call from God to change your life. It is so real that you can't resist the call, and you go up to the altar and enter into the supernatural experience of becoming born-again.

This is what church is supposed to be like – not some stuffy old place where old people sing the Doxology in 4/4 time like a death march, but the electricity of the Holy Ghost flowing through the whole congregation like a river of Life. I have been in services when the power of God came down so strong that the air would shimmer from the glory of God. You would feel like time had stopped, and you had entered into a bubble of hyper-reality.

That's the kind of church we had during the Jesus Movement in the 70s. And you know what the good part is? We would get to do it all over again every night! And we couldn't wait to get there!

We told everyone about it. Nobody escaped us -- on the streets, on buses, in their homes -- we handed out tracts to everyone we met and told them to come to the most exciting event of their lives.

And they came. And came. And came. Every night, 30 to 50 souls would come down to the altar to give their lives to Jesus Christ, and they would go back out to tell others of this incredible experience that had happened to them in a church where every night the divine met humanity and the supernatural became natural.

Fifty years later, I sit and listen to Christians postulate about how wrong traditional church services are, how dead they seem, and how wrong it is for a preacher to stand behind the pulpit and hammer his ideas into the silent congregation before him. They have become so disillusioned by what they have experienced that they are ready to discard the entire notion of Church -- preachers and all – and cut themselves loose from those suffocating old traditions.

They have never seen church the way it's supposed to be, and, not having seen the real thing, it is hard for them to know the difference.

They haven't felt the power of the Holy Ghost thundering across the pulpit driving each and every word into their heart straight from the Throne of God. They haven't seen when even the preacher had no control over what was coming out of his mouth, but God had taken over the service and was preaching the message. They haven't experienced a lifting in the Spirit that rips open the fabric of this reality and takes you right off the face of the Earth into a heavenly realm. They haven't felt the transformation in their lives that only a Holy Ghost-filled service can bring. It's not Church that they object to – it's the staleness of the apostasy that has destroyed American Christianity over the last 50 years.

Revival is about bringing back to life a church that has destroyed herself with the poison of worldly Christianity and, with her last breath, has begged God to please have mercy and revive her once again.

It is, at the same time, the ultimate tragedy and the greatest love story.

Ashes in the Morning

> *"Command Aaron and his sons, saying, This is the law of the burnt offering: It is the burnt offering, because of the burning upon the altar all night unto the morning, and the fire of the altar shall be burning in it.*
>
> *And the priest shall put on his linen garment, and his linen breeches shall he put upon his flesh, and take up the ashes which the fire hath consumed with the burnt offering on the altar, and he shall put them beside the altar.*
>
> *And he shall put off his garments, and put on other garments, and carry forth the ashes without the camp unto a clean place."*
> *(Leviticus 6:9-11)*

I can't help getting a picture in my mind as I read this of those old-fashioned prayer warriors who would take their burden for revival to that secret place in God and burn like fire all night long in a holy sacrifice until they were left prostrate in consecrated hot ashes before the Throne of God in the morning.

One of the hardest things to get across to most churches when I am preaching revival is this concept of deep prevailing prayer that finds an agonizing place of travail before the Throne of God. It is easy to relay the principles of revival. I've practically got all the chapters memorized. I can show anyone the blueprints for revival that God has written into His Word. I can even tell you in passionate terms what the price for revival entails. But what I cannot do is insert that deep abiding burden for souls into someone's heart – the kind of burden that drives you to travailing agony before God. God has to do that.

Throughout history, every revival has been preceded by faithful souls in travailing prayer. This is not the quick and efficient microwave prayers that we are used to. Those are convenient but not effective. Neither is it repetitious chanting asking for the same thing over and over again like a tape recorder. Those prayers lack the passion that drives through the barriers of spiritual warfare that hang over you. No, travailing prayer is like what a woman goes through in childbirth. This is a total commitment of heart, body, mind, and soul in agonizing labor to take hold of the hem of God's robe and bring forth a living child. Revivals are only born from such prayer.

Only those whom God has carefully chosen can fulfill such a calling. It is far too deep and heavy for mere mortal man to bear without the power of God's Holy Spirit. Just as the priests could not carry the Ark of the Covenant without the assistance of the Spirit (2 Sam. 6:13), so these secret warriors are driven to depths of agonizing prayer by the One who has already agonized on Calvary.

When we find sacrificial saints who become so consumed in the fire of prayer that there is nothing left by morning but hot ashes with the coals of fire still in them, then and only then can we expect revival.

This is the heart and soul of true revival – not the showy expositions that the "would-be" revival preachers today are giving us. Yelling "Fire, fire, fire!" does not bring down the fire of God. He is not amused with such cheap antics. Neither is God impressed with your efforts to show how powerful you are by pushing people to the floor to get them to be "slain in the Spirit." Neither will a show of the gift of healing bring repentance to a church that is in a Laodicean complacency and has lost its way.

Many of the big names in today's charismatic movement are more show than substance, more circus than church, or, as Ravenhill put it, more Hollywood than holiness. How can we not be ashamed of our carnal attempts to circumvent the sacrifice that burns us to ashes?

Only travail and agony bring forth birth. God does not deal in C-Sections.

> "Then saith he unto his disciples, The harvest truly is plenteous, but the laborers are few; Pray ye therefore the Lord of the harvest, that he will send forth laborers into his harvest." (Matt. 9:37,38)

No Anointing

"Ye are the salt of the earth: but if the salt have lost his savour, wherewith shall it be salted?" Matthew 5:13

Whenever I have a get-together, I always invite Barry. Barry always adds extra spice to the party. I guess he's sort of half nuts, but the half of him that's nuts is a really fun kind of nuts. He's like the sweet and sour sauce that you put on your egg rolls. You can eat them dry, but without the sauce, it tastes like something is missing.

Church is a lot like that. Oh sure, we have wonderful churches with great pastors and really nice people. And I'm sure you all love your church services. But something is missing.

Ever wonder why so many folks out there are not flocking to your church? And I'm not talking about sinners – I'm talking about Christians! Ask them sometime. You'll find (if you can get past their initial polite responses) that they need something more than what they are finding at church. Something is missing, and they are left hungry when they leave. What is that thing that is missing? It's not the setting or the message or the people. It's difficult to put your finger on, but whatever it is, it is sorely needed to satisfy that hunger that so many people have in the depths of their souls.

I brought my family just recently to a service where someone who I knew was a real servant of the Lord was preaching. And it was good … sort of. All the right theological elements were in place, the preachers said a lot of great stuff, and it was good to be there. But something was missing.

As we drove home, my wife pointed right to it – there was no anointing. Great message, wonderful preachers, nice place … but no anointing. Egg rolls without sauce.

Now I'm sure that a whole bunch of you are going to say, "But oh, we have the anointing in _our_ services!" Then why are hundreds of souls not flocking to your altar to get saved every week?

Think that's excessive? Back in the '70s, we had 30 to 50 souls at the altar _every_ night and _twice_ on Sunday! And it was because the power of the Holy Spirit was literally pouring out on us every night, drawing hungry souls from everywhere.

If you haven't been saved long enough to have experienced the revivals in the early '70s, then you have no idea what you're missing. If you weren't there for the Brush Arbor revivals, then all you have to compare your services to are the narratives that were written by those who were there. We have not seen anything like it for 50 years. One exception would be the Brownsville Revival in the '90s.

Once you have tasted of a Holy Ghost anointing, you will never be the same, and you will never again be satisfied with "church as usual." It is the sweet and sour sauce to your egg roll services; it's the salt that flavors the meal that you are serving to saved and unsaved alike. It's the thing that draws souls to the altar in droves. It's the very essence of the Spirit of God.

And it is missing.

So, what do we need to do to get it back? I am sure that everybody's loaded up on volumes of Christian self-help books written by every pseudo-expert who has a new "word from God" to tell the rest of us.

And maybe that's the problem. We're so busy trying to figure it out that we're not letting God take control. Maybe if we threw out our prepared messages and burned our theological books, we could be free to follow the leading of the Holy Ghost. But no, we're afraid to do that. We have to do our programmed Christianity according to the way we've been taught to do it. God brought us to the dance, but we want to lead the way we learned at Arthur Murray's Dance Class, so instead of waltzing with grace, we end up stepping on His toes.

When we are ready to admit our failure, God will be more than ready to pour out His anointing on us again, even more than what we have experienced in the past. I have always said that the way to victory is through surrender; the way to wholeness is through brokenness; the way to God is through repentance.

Let's start there and see where it leads.

Four R's

Something is wrong in the Church today.

I don't say that lightly, or as someone who thrives on criticizing everyone else just to establish my spiritual superiority or as someone with sour grapes because things aren't the way I would like them. I say it because of how many people I meet daily who are discouraged by the traditional church and have chosen not to attend anymore.

Everywhere I turn, I hear people complaining about the same thing. This isn't something localized to a particular area or limited to a certain denomination -- I hear this from all sorts of people, many with impeccable spiritual credentials. Oftentimes I hear from pastors who have spent decades in ministry who are now questioning the vibrancy of the Church. Others are just kids off the streets, armed with little more than a spiritual hunger, who refuse to attend church, not because they don't believe but because they are repelled by what they see.

No matter how you view this issue, no matter what position you have, and no matter what church you belong to, you have to admit that something is wrong. We are supposed to be the salt of the Earth, as something that gives flavor to make a meal taste good. But when we are not attracting the lost but rather repelling them, then our salt has lost its savor. What makes it even worse is that we are even repelling the saved.

There are opposing extremes to this issue, true, but shouldn't the middle be closer to the truth? We see, on the one hand, the churches that are so loose and "loving" that they excuse any sin or misconduct, including homosexuality and adultery in the church. On the other hand, there are those who, in their religious zeal, have taken it upon themselves to proclaim their self-righteous judgments on every church around them. Somewhere they read that the Word of God is a hammer that breaks the rock in pieces, so they've traded in their fishing pole for a sledgehammer.

But in the middle, where we hope to find something more balanced, we find a modern church that is socially-based, smooth and sensual, sophisticated, and presented as a Hollywood production so that it will appeal to the crowds that flock there. Listen, if it walks like a duck, quacks like a duck, and looks like a duck, then it is most likely a duck and not a church.

And what, may I ask, ever happened to the Gospel of power? If our churches are supposed to be so good, then why are so many people turned off by them? If the fire that is burning in our churches was from off the altar of God instead of a Wizard of Oz production, then I can guarantee you that hungry souls would be drawn by the Spirit of God, but instead, they are turning away. Something is wrong!

Where are the old-fashioned preachers who used to preach under an anointing of power and relied, not on their stack of disheveled notes, but on the power of God to deliver the message? Our pastors today follow the social and marketing formulas they were taught in college and present a Gospel in a multi-media fashion with five bulleted points, a poem, and three jokes. Something is wrong!

What happened to the strong calls for repentance that brought thousands down to the altar to repent and ask Jesus Christ to save their souls? This is the litmus test for Christianity. It is the essence of the Cross and the Great Commission that Jesus commanded us with. If the church is not winning souls, then she is a barren woman, and it is a shame unto her. Something is wrong!

Where did all the miracles go? Not the weak excuses of "if it is God's will ...," or reliance on a "gradual healing" while you raise one hand raised in prayer for healing while you hold a doctor's appointment in the other, but the instant manifestation of the power of God? Jesus said to heal the sick and preach the Gospel. Was He just kidding? Did He really mean it? Yes, He meant it! If there is not a flowing of miracle healings in your church, then I'm sorry, something is wrong!

Where is the outpouring of the Holy Ghost? Do we even know what it means anymore to feel the presence of the Spirit of God descend on a service and fill up the room with holiness? Or do we think that our party excitement when someone plays a cool song or when some charismatic speaker works the crowd is the Holy Ghost? It's been so long since we've seen the real thing that we don't even know what it is anymore. Something is wrong!

Something of deep substance is missing in our church today. But we've become so sophisticated and enamored with our social Gospel that we don't even realize that something is wrong. We are left like Gideon, threshing his wheat in secret by the winepress of God because our fields have been taken over by a worldly church. And we wonder out loud to the angel, "What happened to the miracles our fathers have told us about?"

Yeah, that's my question too. What happened?

When we lose our fear of God, we lose our power in God. And at that point, as it says in Isaiah 29, the Book became sealed unto us so that we no longer even grasp how far we have fallen. We read it, but we can't see past the surface of the page because wisdom is determined by the fear of God.

I believe in the four R's, the four steps to revival – Recognition, Repentance, Righteousness, and Revival. The first step to Revival is to realize that we don't have one, to recognize that something is desperately wrong with our churches and that we have lost something precious in our pursuit of a super-sophisticated modern Church. We've lost it, and we need to get it back.

Only when we finally acknowledge our sin can we begin the journey back to the place God has reserved for us.

> " And unto the angel of the church of the Laodiceans write; These things saith the Amen, the faithful and true witness, the beginning of the creation of God; I know thy works, that thou art neither cold nor hot: I would thou wert cold or hot. So then because thou art

lukewarm, and neither cold nor hot, I will spue thee out of my mouth.

Because thou sayest, I am rich, and increased with goods, and have need of nothing; and knowest not that thou art wretched, and miserable, and poor, and blind, and naked: I counsel thee to buy of me gold tried in the fire, that thou mayest be rich; and white raiment, that thou mayest be clothed, and that the shame of thy nakedness do not appear; and anoint thine eyes with eyesalve, that thou mayest see.

As many as I love, I rebuke and chasten: be zealous therefore, and repent."

Revelations 3:14-19

Feelings

Well, once again, I have been told that I was going to Hell.

This time from someone who had read the Statement of Faith on my website, Revivalfire.org, and decided that I was not saved because I do not believe in Eternal Security. The funny thing is, this was from a person who believes that once you are saved, you are always saved, no matter what you do.

So, which is it? Sorry lady, but you can't have it both ways.

She was also quick to point out that you cannot go by feelings. I beg your pardon, but I don't see how you can go <u>without</u> feelings.

Yes, we walk by Faith, and we must go by the Word of God, but don't the Spirit and the Word agree? And isn't faith the substance of things hoped for? And if it is a substance, can you not feel it? Faith opens the door to walk into the presence of God, but believe me, when you are in the presence of God, you can feel it!

I don't want to just believe I'm saved or think I'm saved. I want to know it! I want to feel it! I love that rush that comes down from the Throne of God when I pray. When I raise my hands and lift up my heart in praise and feel the Heavens open up – wow, there is no feeling in the world like that!

When you lead someone through the Sinner's Prayer, and you feel the Spirit of God come down and flow through them – how can you not feel that?

When you lay hands on someone that is sick and feel the Blood of Jesus Christ wash over them and heal them right in front of you; when the preacher is under the Anointing and you feel the power of God flowing through the whole church; when you are deep in prayer, and the Lord speaks to you or shows you a vision – tell me, how can you not go by feelings?

Perhaps that woman has never felt the supernatural power of the Holy Ghost in her life. If she did, maybe she'd have a different opinion.

I'll tell you what, if I were in a church, and I couldn't feel the Spirit of God, then I have to believe that something is missing. (Like maybe God?) If you cannot feel the Spirit of God, then something is standing between you and Him. Maybe that something is your religion.

I don't want a cold, dead faith. I don't want to guess or try to theologically convince myself that I'm saved. My faith isn't cerebral; it's deep in my heart. I want a relationship with the Lord that is so personal and powerful that all the devils in Hell cannot convince me that I am not right with God. Not even some zealot that doesn't agree with me.

In order to be led by the Spirit of God and keep heading down the right path with Him, you have got to be able to feel His leading and His correction. This is not something you can guess on or gamble your soul on the throw of a dice – you have to be sure. Hell burns for a long time.

Jesus said that as many as are led by the Spirit, they are the Sons of God.

And if you're not led by the Spirit … well, good luck trying to figure it out.

Another World

I had a wonderful experience this morning that I'd like to share with you. As we were reading Bible, my little girl asked about Noah. She remembered that last week we had read about how Noah walked with God.

"How do you walk with God, Daddy? And how do you know when you are walking with Him?"

In the course of a careful explanation, we touched on the fact that there are two worlds – the world we live in that we can see around us and the spiritual world that we can't see.

I explained to her how God is a Spirit and that our souls will leave our bodies someday to be with God.

"You mean it's like being in a car, but we're not really the car; we're just inside it?"

I watched as the idea of two distinct realities dawned across her face. Her eyes got as big as silver dollars as the stark realization hit her of the existence of another whole world in the Spirit.

So that's where God is!

How easy it is for us to forget. Sometimes we get so wrapped in our daily lives that we lose that focus. But He is always there, isn't He? And one of these days, the covering that is cast upon all people will be ripped away, and we will see Life as it really is – simply a test for entering into Eternity.

I want to be like Noah, who not only believed in God but walked every day, conscious that God was right by his side. What a confidence there is in walking with a Savior who is right there beside you, who hears your every prayer and watches your every step.

There is no valley, trial, or tribulation that you cannot go through when you know you are walking with the Lord God Almighty. You have the power to overcome all things, and you fear nothing when you fear God and place your trust in Him.

Ah, but how do you walk with God, Daddy? That's the real question, isn't it?

If you don't know the answer, you need to make an altar before God and ask Jesus Christ to wash away all your sins in His blood, confess Him as the Son of God who died and rose again that you might have Life, and ask him to save your soul. Only then will your eyes be opened, and you will feel the Spirit of Life enter into you.

...and then you will know.

I know one little 9-year-old girl who will be spending the next few days pondering that whole concept,

At least until next week when she has another question.

A Little Girl Named Hope

It was midnight when my daughter, Kelly, called. I was alone on the porch outside praying, just God and me.

I had been wrestling in prayer for God to rip out all the ugly stuff that was buried deep in my heart. I had felt for some time that I had hit a brick wall in my spiritual life that God just wasn't going to let me get around. It was as if God had turned off my motor, and I was stuck – I wasn't even idling. I had come to a complete stop, and I wasn't going anywhere.

Over the past several years, the Lord has allowed me to do some remarkable things. I was so excited! I had done things that I never thought I would have ever been able to do. Not only had I been able to do them, but I had witnessed the incredible power of God flowing through me during those times. I felt like I was getting to do some great things and had finally come into the ministry that I had been waiting for all my life. I felt like I was running full tilt at 150 mph.

And then He clamped down hard.

I could feel it before I could see it. Something was missing. That feeling of confidence was eroding, and things weren't happening for me like they used to. I had seen many miracles and healings, and had gotten special words from God, but now there was silence. Dead silence. If I prayed for someone, nothing happened. Doors started closing around me, and I felt like I was out in the middle of a desert.

Now, I've been through the desert before, so I figured this was just another growing time, but this time it felt different. I don't know how to describe the feeling, but it was as if something was blocking my way—something I couldn't see. I kept trying to dismiss it, but it was there no matter what I tried to do. I began to realize that it wasn't something external – it was me.

I felt like my pride had caused me to be such a failure that I might have lost whatever calling I had in God and very possibly would never again feel the anointing flow through me over the pulpit or through my hands when praying over others. But that was okay. I was ready to surrender my place to someone else who would be much better than I had been. I was resolved to accept whatever lowly position God granted me, whether it was sweeping the floor, or cleaning the toilets for the saints – it didn't matter. I just wanted to serve the Lord. I surrendered my pride and asked for forgiveness.

There's a place where we sometimes have to go to that is far away from the outside world – a quiet place deep inside you where everything around you stops. Like the Garden of Gethsemane, you have to go there alone, taking nothing with you but your raw, naked soul. It is there where you strip away everything you hold onto, every crutch that you hang onto for support, and all the lofty ideas that you have of yourself so that you become stripped down and naked before God. It is the place where you come to a realization of who you really are before God and accept the searing humility that we are nothing but dust and ashes, and He is God.

I was in that place when my daughter called.

A little girl she knew had just been in an accident and was not going to make it. Her name was Hope. My daughter wanted me to pray for God to restore that little girl back to life because she thought God would hear my prayers. At that moment, I didn't know if God would hear me or not. Seriously. I felt as low as I had felt in a long time. But we prayed anyway.

Almost right away, the Spirit of God crashed down on both of us like a lightning bolt! I was so excited that I was jumping and dancing all over the porch, shouting and praising the Lord. It was midnight, but I didn't care what the neighbors thought. God had answered – really answered -- and I believed He was going to raise that girl from the dead!

Two days later, however, the hospital still had the girl on life support -- not dead, but not alive. I cried out to God, wondering what happened, and a little voice went off in the back of my head, "She's still alive, isn't she?" Amen, Lord, she's still alive. Maybe God was waiting for an opportune time or something. Surely, He would raise her up now and show the world that He is still sitting on the Throne and still answers prayer.

But that night, she died.

I don't get it. What happened? We felt the power of the Holy Spirit crash down on us. God, I thought You were going to heal her! Did I not pray hard enough or long enough? Did I quit too soon just because I got such an immediate answer? Or was it me? Would I have taken credit for her healing and strutted around about how powerful I was in God? Why did God allow her to die?

You can imagine how devastated I was. Maybe I was as bad as I thought I was. Maybe it was my fault. Maybe God couldn't heal her because of me.

But, you know, sometimes it's not about you. It doesn't matter how much stuff you know, how good you are at doing anything, or what a failure you have been. The world doesn't hinge on your performance or how significant your accomplishments are. God is not limited by your limitations.

The next day, as I was dragging myself through my discouragement, I got a picture from the Lord. It wasn't much, just a glimpse. But it was enough. I could see Jesus standing up high, overlooking the world, and standing beside Him with His arm wrapped around her was that little girl. They stood at that place between this life and the next, on the edge of Eternity, with the entrance to Heaven behind them, and He was asking her if she wanted to go back to Earth.

"No," she said. "I want to stay here with you, Jesus."

"Yes," He said as He hugged her a little closer. "I want you to stay here with Me, too."

And they both turned and walked into the gates of Heaven.

There is more to this story.

Almost exactly one year later, my daughter was in an accident, and we rushed to be with her at the hospital. One of her friends had heard about the accident and was there with us. For some reason, even though I had not thought about it for a year, I began to tell this woman the story about Hope. She burst into tears. "I knew it! I knew it all along!"

This woman was Hope's mother. She relayed to me that all of Hope's bones had been crushed, but somehow in the hospital, they had all been healed. All of them! Hope should have survived, but for some reason, she did not. As a mother, this woman knew why. She had told others, but no one believed her, but she knew her little girl.

It was never about me. It was about her. Hope <u>chose</u> to go with Jesus.

Hell

How do you put a value on the concept of Hell? The whole idea is beyond what we can comprehend or grasp. We can't understand Eternity, never mind spending it in the torments of the fires of Hell.

So, we have a solution for it. We just don't think about it.

Maybe if we push it off to the edge of our thoughts, it will go away. But shoving Hell off into the background does not make it go away any more than rationalizing our sins makes them any less sinful. It might fade away from our consciousness, but its stark reality will come into sharp focus when we die.

Surely, Hell is for someone else, not us. Let's concentrate on all the good stuff and convince ourselves that damnation is a dramatization by extremists. Certainly, there are plenty of lukewarm pastors out there who will conciliate our consciences and tell us not to worry.

We're Christians, aren't we? We go to church. We believe in Jesus. Isn't that enough?

Or are we like those who complained that they had eaten and drank in his presence and had done many wonderful works, even prophesied in his name, but were told that He never knew them? (Luke 13:26; Matt.7:23; Ezekiel 18:24)

Oh, but surely that doesn't apply to us, does it? That's for somebody else.

The funny thing is, the very people we think will wind up in Hell think that we are the ones who will wind up there. Maybe we're both right.

Hell has become a four-lettered word and is not supposed to be repeated in polite company. It's kinda like that other nasty word, Fear. You just don't say those things, especially in church, because you will surely offend someone.

Exactly. The preaching of the Cross is an offense to the unsaved (1 Corinthians 1:18).

We live in a world where everything is nice and warm and fuzzy and where everybody is going to Heaven – or so it seems. And that's pretty much the point, isn't it? Nobody, especially pastors, wants to be some critical, judgmental cranky old sourpuss. We just want to "love on people." So we don't tell them the truth, we don't warn them of judgment to come, and we don't take a stand.

Sure. Just ask anybody. They'll tell you. They believe in God, so naturally, they're going to Heaven when they die. Know anybody that doesn't think like that?

Unfortunately, according to the Bible, most people are heading for destruction (Matthew 7:13) – and they don't even know it.

Okay, so I'm a judgmental, cranky ol' sourpuss, but I know that the Bible requires a level of intensity that most of us don't want to admit to. And yet it is all written there in black and white. We just have to read it with open hearts.

As I have often said, 10,000 years from now, you are going to be somewhere. Better make sure there are no rude surprises in store for you when you die. There's no coming back to do it over again.

> *"Strive to enter in at the strait gate: for many, I say unto you, will seek to enter in, and shall not be able."* Luke 13:24

Noah's Seven Days

"But Noah found grace in the eyes of the Lord" Genesis 6:8

On Sunday morning, my two girls wanted to read about Noah. It's a cute story with lots of animals and rainbows. They've seen all the pictures of a chubby old Noah in his brown robe and sandals, looking over the side of the boat with all the friendly animals crowded around him. Such a fun story!

Of course, the reality of it all was much different. It was a time of severe trials, persecution, hardship, and death. I'm sure Noah would never want to go through it again.

One passage stood out to us as we were reading. Noah and his family were in that boat for seven days before the first drop of water fell. I wouldn't be surprised if that period of seven days wasn't the hardest time for them out of the whole ordeal.

Noah had been a preacher of righteousness to a world of scorners and must have been the most unpopular man on the face of the Earth. Nobody likes to hear that they are going to Hell, and I'm sure his generation was no different. It wasn't that they didn't know about God. They were only a handful of generations away from Adam and Eve. It's just that they did not want to give up sin and figured that, somehow, they would be able to get away with it.

We've all heard the Cosby-type jokes about how much jeering Noah must have suffered. After all, for 100 years, all he had to show for his faith was a boat in the backyard. To the rest of the world, that was a huge monument to folly. But Noah believed God and moved with fear to construct that Ark of Safety.

And then came the word to enter the Ark. Seven long days, cooped up with all those animals. No ventilation, no sunlight … and no rain.

I can just imagine the echo of the howls of laughter coming from outside the boat. The old fool had cooped up his family inside that smelly monstrosity, and now he was locked in. But inside, the feeling of anticipation must have been thick and heavy.

Tell me you wouldn't have been wondering during those seven days.

Why wait another seven days? Why couldn't God have just flipped the switch as soon as they got inside? Why this final test of faith? Hadn't they endured enough?

We see this same pattern with God several times throughout the Bible. After everything you've gone through, there is often one more final challenge of faith to overcome before you get the final victory.

Faith in God is not determined by what you know or what you have seen. It is never a matter of how many miracles or personal experiences you have had with God. You cannot count on former victories or things that you have done in the past. Your faith is measured by where you are in God today.

Faith is built in your heart by a continuous determination to seek the face of God each and every day, and like a flame in your heart, it goes out when it runs out of fuel.

Many times, I have heard people say that they believe in God and even bolster it by pointing to their church attendance, but when times of severe tribulation and testing come, how often they fail because all they had was a faith in name only.

Because faith comes by hearing the Word of God (Romans 10:17), immersing yourself in the Word of God will give you the power to pray – not just muttering a bunch of empty words, but real, heart-wrenching prayer. That takes you higher into the Spirit of the Lord and, in turn, deeper into the Word of God. And that builds your faith – one step at a time. Do you think you can accomplish the same things by skimming the Bible in a year? Or throwing God some casual requests when you've got the time?

No, only a driven heart that will seek the face of God will be able to receive the faith to stand in the times when you will need it the most.

Noah had that kind of faith because he relentlessly sought the face of God. And it carried him and his family like a solid rock through those final seven days.

Finding God

Every once in a while, I hear of someone who "found" God. Now, we all know that it wasn't God that was lost; it was us.

Now how can that be, seeing that everywhere you look, you find all kinds of churches, books, and even movies that talk about Jesus Christ? Is no one paying attention, or is it all just a bunch of white noise to an unbeliever?

I was once such a lost soul. I heard all about Jesus Christ as a kid growing up, but I could not believe it. It was all such a fantastic story to me that stretched the limits of my belief. It wasn't that no one tried. They even brought a local pastor into my schoolroom to try and convince me that the gospel was the Truth, but he left even more frustrated than I.

Let's face it; this is a pretty incredible story. First, God picks a small group of people and tells them what He wants. They can't seem to get it together to follow His instructions and end up with a bizarre version of what God wanted. To try and salvage the deal, God sends his prophets to reprove them and show them the true way, but they kill them because these prophets aren't telling them what they want to hear.

I'm OK so far. This all makes sense to me since I understand that God has morals, and we don't. Given free license, our flesh will always go after lust, pride, and self-gratification. We might acknowledge that God is there, but there is always that struggle inside us to sin. And since God created us, He must want us to do what is right, and it makes sense that He would send messengers to warn us and pull us back into the right way.

Now comes the tricky part. God has a Son. If you look back into the Old Testament, you can see the references to God's Son in a ton of places. But why, oh why, would He send His Son to come down here in the flesh? On top of that, He knows that we will kill him. What's more, that is all part of the Plan!

Boy, that's pretty tough to swallow. I mean, would you do that? I sure wouldn't.

OK. So, God has got a bigger heart than we do. I can believe that, but wow, that is a whole lot bigger than I can imagine! Nevertheless, a lot of people have the innate ability to believe all this by faith. Me? I couldn't swallow it. That was just a bit more than I could handle.

I used to have a saying in those days (that I must admit I would spit out with some swagger) that if God is so big, how come He doesn't come down and show us? I believed in the things I could see, feel, and touch, but please, am I supposed to give up all my fun for something I can't see?

And then I found God.

Or rather, He found me.

It wasn't some intelligent theological dissertation by some idiot with a Ph.D., or some placid-faced, goody-two-shoes with a Howdy Dowdy grin that convinced me. I wasn't impressed with heart-swelling pleas that God loved me or hollow arguments that somebody had to have created the world around me, so God must be there. And please, don't tell me that I should be good because it's good to be good.

No, it was the power of God that knocked me out. I didn't want to be good; I didn't want to be saved from my sins, and, from what I'd seen, I sure didn't want to be a Christian. But it's tough to dismiss the idea of God when you can feel the power of the Holy Spirit crashing down on you.

It only took an instant to realize that if God was really there – like really really! -- then there was most likely a Hell for guys like me. That was rather chilling.

I decided to make the jump of faith and ask Jesus Christ to save my soul. After all, what could I lose? If He was really there, then I figured I would know it. If He wasn't, then no big deal; I'd just go on my way.

But He was there. What an incredible experience! Why didn't anybody ever tell me that Salvation was such an amazing experience and that you would stand up on your feet with an understanding that you had never felt before? I had finally found God! What an idiot I had been all my life!

I listen with sadness today, so many years later, to all the Christian apologetics, all the theological analysts, and all the efforts to explain the Truth of the Gospel in carnal terms. It's like listening to Christian salesmen trying to sell you a used car. And I think back to those days when they tried to convince me with all that white noise.

It is only the power of God that wins souls, nothing else. Analyze the Gospel down to the head of a pin, and all you will end up with is a story that is hard to believe. But, oh, reach out and touch the power of God, and that will make all the difference in the world!

And that's where you will find God.

Grasp of God

There's something great and vast about Life that eludes me. Often we try to pierce the veil of this reality with feelings and emotions that are thrust out of our souls like spears into the night in an attempt to touch that ethereal something that barely escapes the fingertips of our souls.

We call it searching for Truth, but the idea is always so nebulous. We use words to wrap something tangible around those feelings and paint them into something that we can grasp, but some things can never be roped to anything rock solid. There's more to life than we can ever understand.

We think we know, but it is all beyond our comprehension and much bigger than we can imagine. We all have a concept of what God is, how big He is, and where He resides, but it is only translucent glimmers in our souls. Somewhere, way up there, is God. We feel that if we could just slice into the fabric of Reality with a knife, we would see Him sitting on His throne surrounded by all those angels, but we don't have anything sharp enough.

So we try to bring it all into focus with words, vaguely aware of how impotent our efforts are. Still, we try because somewhere down deep inside us is an urgency that knows that Eternity is waiting for us at the end of our lives. Somewhere on the other side of that dark door of death, our ultimate destiny awaits us, silently, patiently, and immovable. We can feel it, but we can't quite put our finger on it. We try to grasp it, but our fingers come back empty.

Wasn't it Thoreau who said, "Most men lead lives of quiet desperation"? Life in this reality is absorbing but transient. Our time seems to be spent in a sea of long pauses that are filled with work or amusement while we wait for those intermittent islands of something truly meaningful. Not that love, charity, fun, or any of the other things of life that we value are vain, but every once in a while, we are able to reach through that veil and touch something eternal. Sometimes, it is just for a moment, but it is enough to realize that we have a fleeting grasp on something that transcends this world.

A friend of mine said that there's more to God than what we want. Just as God is greater than what we can want, so is life much more than what we can see. I want to finish the course of my life knowing that I have at least touched some islands of true reality and not gone through my life numb to my eternal destiny. If God is true, then being able to touch the Throne of God is the only real thing that we can do. To dismiss that as a secondary interest is to miss the meaning of Life.

We pass through the road of Life only once, and then Death slams the door shut behind us. Reach through the veil and go through life with your fingers grasped around the hand of God.

The Deal with Hell

What is the deal with Hell? Is it really there or not? And if it is there, is it as bad as we have been led to believe? And (here's the real question) if it is as bad as they say, why are we not more terrified?

I came to Christ as a non-believer – I didn't believe in God, didn't believe in Jesus, I didn't believe in Heaven, and I sure didn't believe in Hell. And I didn't want to, either. But when I got saved and felt the Spirit of God transform me, I accepted the whole deal. I didn't need to see it; it was part of the whole package. If it was written in the Bible, that was good enough for me.

But the rational, analytical part of me has always looked curiously at the whole idea of Heaven and Hell. It just doesn't make sense. While I accept it wholeheartedly, it sure would be nice if I could get a glimpse of it (just to make sure). I've listened to people who have seen either Heaven or Hell, and when listening to them tell the vision, I can see in their intensity and depth that they really did see these things. But I'd still like to see it for myself.

But that's not how it works, does it? God doesn't offer us great descriptions in vivid details about these two places. If God was a real estate agent for a vacation resort in Heaven, He'd most likely go broke. He just doesn't tell us that much. Instead of focusing on the destination, God is more concerned with the journey.

Sure, everybody wants to go to Heaven, so we focus on that, all the while convincing ourselves that we are going there someday. I've even heard that all dogs go to Heaven. How? Well, that doesn't matter as much to us as the self-assurance that, most certainly, we will go there. Plus, all our friends will be there. Have you ever heard someone proclaim at a funeral that their deceased friend is most assuredly burning in Hell right now? No, we all believe we are going to Heaven because we have merely focused on the destination and have dismissed the journey.

Hell, on the other hand, is a place that we believe is reserved only for really, really bad people, the monsters of our society. The rest of us aren't that bad – oh, sure, we have a few basic character flaws, but hey, God loves us, and He understands. Yeah, I'm sure He does.

Perhaps if we put the whole idea behind us, the stark reality of Hell would just go away. We can worry about it later. In the meantime, we all have our lives before us and that looms more in our consciousness than some ethereal specter of a place of torment that we haven't seen with our eyes or measured with our scientific instruments. Preachers that attempt to burst our rosy bubble with a message about Hell are derided as hateful and critical. We don't believe that they understand God's love, but instead, try to force us into an ascetic lifestyle by using fear tactics. Heard that before, have you?

Now, I'm not sure which preachers they are referring to, because, in 50 years of ministry, I have not found hardly any of them. Where are all these hellfire and brimstone preachers they are talking about? Or is that just an excuse we use to dismiss what we do not want to face?

But what if? If Heaven is supposed to be so much better than we can imagine, what if Hell is far worse than what we can fear? What if it really is there, and the countless souls who ignored it are now there screaming in agony right now?

I have long said that Hell is the most prevalent reality there is – much more than anything else. Why? Because Jesus said that most people are going to end up there (Matt. 7:14). Certainly, if God dug a hole just outside our city limits where we could see all the way down to the pits of Hell, there would be many of us standing on the edge of that chasm with a much different perspective on their lives. But He has not. He has left it up to us to choose.

I have said that people will believe what they want to believe in spite of the facts… and they will use the Bible to justify it. As an old friend once told me, "People will follow their hearts." How true. A sweet message of the "Good Ship Lollipop" is much more appealing than the stark realities of eternal judgment. With a quick sweep to push those realities behind us, sin appears less sinful and holiness less compulsory.

But what if God really did mean exactly what He said? What if He has used our vanities as the filter to separate the wheat from the chaff, as He says in Isaiah 30:28? What if our choice of destination isn't what determines our fate but our choice of the path that leads us there?

"Enter ye in at the strait gate: for wide is the gate, and broad is the way, that leadeth to destruction, and many there be which go in thereat: Because strait is the gate, and narrow is the way, which leadeth unto life, and few there be that find it. Matthew 7:13,14

Mercy

"Mercy and truth preserve the king: and his throne is upholden by mercy." (Prov. 20:28)

If there is one message that can be deemed the most important of all, it is the message of mercy. The Apostle Paul wrote that charity is even more important than faith and hope, the two pillars that our salvation rests upon.

It is not enough to be righteous before God. The Pharisees were so righteous that they were squeaky clean, and yet they wound up in Hell. It is to those who are merciful that God will show Himself merciful, not the righteous. Mercy is at the core of God's personality. Without it, He would have empty mansions in Heaven with no one to fill them.

And yet, I constantly hear Christians drone on about all the right doctrines that they believe in and the things they have done for the Lord. Their conversation always seems to center around themselves, but when is it going to be about others?

The Gospel of Jesus Christ is not about you. It will never be about you. It is about others. If you never grasp this, you will never understand the Cross. Jesus didn't die so we could be blessed, have a good time in the Lord, and attend a wonderful church – He died to save sinners, and He commanded us to do the same.

Revival starts with the merciful. The forerunners who contended for hours of travail on their knees long before the fire of revival ever fell were not praying for themselves – they were crying out to God for the lost. Those hours of crying and wells of tears spring from a fountain whose source is that blessed burden for lost souls. No revival comes without the sacrifice of these faithful warriors.

Where does that burden come from? From prayer itself. You have to ask God to give it to you before you can ever have the strength to drive past your flesh and self-will to contend with that kind of intensity. No human willpower is enough to overcome the spiritual barriers that Satan throws up before these saints. This is a battle of spiritual power, not flesh and blood. Only the power of God can press this kind of burden upon us to take us up, through, and over this kind of warfare. We are victors only through the Blood of Jesus and the power of God.

When we ask God to give us a burden for lost souls, it starts the process that leads to revival. This is where it always begins, for no revival will ever take place without a core of prayer warriors burdened with this weight to rip through the skies and bring down the fire from the Altar of God.

But you have to ask for it because we are not born with it. It is contrary to human nature. You have to have a desire for the desire; you have to want to want; you have to deny yourself and ask for the Cross. But when you ask, you are asking for God's own burden, and He will give it liberally to those who sincerely ask. That burden is the God-given essence of His own heart, and it is planted in our hearts by Him alone. But you have to ask.

When we pray for a deep, overwhelming burden for the lost, God will reveal the stark reality of Hell to us. Until then, we are numb to the realities of Eternity. When the veil is ripped away from our fleshly understanding, and we see with eternal clarity the extent of the torments of everlasting destruction and the rock-solid assurance of judgment, the focus of our entire world forever changes. Nothing else matters – not money, blessings, peace, or any of this world's entertainments or comforts, and certainly not ourselves. The enormity of Hell and judgment looms before us and dominates everything we see.

This is the thing that drives us to labor in the furnace of God's prayer room with inexhaustible fervor. This is what births revival: charity, mercy, and a burden for lost souls. Without that, we are nothing but a tinkling cymbal and a sounding brass, taken with our vain jangling in a desire to be wise and righteous. For revival to come, we must take our focus off ourselves and put it on others. That is the essence of the Spirit of Jesus Christ, the true meaning of the Cross, and the heart of God.

I fear this is the dividing line between the sheep and the goats. Belief in God, doctrinal integrity, and church attendance will not get you into Heaven. He is looking for something in your heart that transcends the flesh and brings you into the presence of God. That thing is mercy.

"He that dwelleth in the secret place of the most High shall abide under the shadow of the Almighty." Psalms 91:1

Humpty Dumpty

> *"For my people have committed two evils; they have forsaken me the fountain of living waters, and hewed them out cisterns, broken cisterns, that can hold no water." Jeremiah 2:13*

Lately, I've been attending a Bible reading group at a church that I had never thought I would visit. Their requests for discipleship from their pastor had gained no traction, so out of hunger and desperation, they formed their own reading group. They asked me to attend because they had read my booklet on Four Steps to Revival and felt that I had something to offer.

I was surprised to find a genuine hunger for God in these people that I would have thought had dried up long ago. There is no demonstrated move of the Holy Spirit in this particular denomination but rather an adherence to archaic liturgies and formal worship repeated each week out of a book of prayers that was written centuries ago. And yet their hunger still pushes up through the arid ground of a church that has remained fallow for longer than anyone can remember.

Although they welcome me with open arms, I am still a "Pentecostal," a distant cousin of what they are used to. To them, Pentecost is considered an anomaly that has sprung up on the fringes of the Christian faith. How odd that sounds from my perspective! It's as if they look at Pentecostals as certain elements of Christendom that had chosen a different, more unusual form of worship that was acceptable, but not mainstream.

But we didn't choose Pentecost. Pentecost chose us. The outpouring of the Holy Ghost was not roped in like a wayward steer into our corral – God roped us into His corral, lassoed with the ropes of His Spirit. An outpouring of a true revival of the Spirit of God can not be manufactured or theologically created. It is prayed in with a desperation that is pressed into our souls by a God who is yearning for His people to return unto Him. Revival is something that descends from God so that prayers can ascend back to Him so that

He can, in turn, bring down an outpouring to rescue the people of God who are starving.

I listened to these folks proudly repeat how their bishop had encouraged them against the homosexual encroachment on their church. Their denomination had been severely attacked by an element that introduced homosexuality into their priesthood, even consecrating actively gay bishops. They hope that if they do not raise too much of a fuss against this liberal intrusion of the Gay agenda, the storm will pass over them, and their church will not be taken away from them. In other words, if we just don't provoke the devil, maybe he will leave us alone.

Words of encouragement are fine, but words alone do little if not delivered under the anointed power of the Holy Ghost. And like Gideon, I wondered where the manifestation of that power was in their ancient communion. Where are the signs that Jesus said would follow His believers?

I wondered when the last time this bishop had laid hands on the sick and seen them recover right before his eyes. I mused that, had I asked that question out loud, they would probably have asked me in retort when was the last time that I had. Well, it was a few weeks ago. And not just one, but a whole line of people coming up to the altar for healing, every one of whom got healed. And what about my church? Had it ever raised the dead? Well, yes, just a few months ago, we had a man who was clinically brain-dead and was about to have the plug pulled on his life support. We stormed the Throne of God for him, and just before they pulled the plug, he popped up out of bed, as alive and well as he had been before he had been sick.

Why do people hang on to dead forms of worship when God has so much life to offer if they would just humble themselves and let go of their old carnal ways? Is there something in human nature that makes us afraid to let go and allow ourselves to fall into His hands? Are we so stuck in our generational conventions that we have forgotten to walk in a yielded faith? Is the certainty of the tangible institution of church more adhesive than an abstract trust in the Spirit of God? What are they hanging onto?

As always, our direction comes from the Word of God. The law that God gave in Leviticus 14 for infected houses, including houses of God, was to get out of the house and then scour it for all forms of leprosy, whether that be sin or any form of heresy. If the house cannot be healed, then everything that has been left in the house was to be taken outside the camp and burned. So a church that has leprosy found in it should be scoured. If it cannot be healed, then get out lest you be destroyed along with it.

When we content ourselves with the old wineskins of the status quo in the face of manifest obsolescence, we choose to forsake the Living Waters and hang on to broken cisterns that can hold no water. We may have a form of church and a glimmer of righteousness, but when we forsake the power thereof, we leave ourselves with nothing to cement those broken cisterns back together again. Like Humpty Dumpty, a church that has had a great fall cannot be put together again.

The time is coming soon when Satan will promote his false ecumenical church to bring the entire world into his fold. His minions will do great wonders, even calling down fire from heaven, and all that are upon the Earth will worship him. If the leprosy that infects the churches to join this one-world religion cannot be cleansed, will we still adhere to our traditions and not rouse ourselves from our convenience to revive a faith that is not based upon theological conventions but on the raw Spirit of God?

"And I heard another voice from heaven, saying, Come out of her, my people, that ye be not partakers of her sins, and that ye receive not of her plagues." (Rev 18:4)

The Harvest is Past

> *"For I know the thoughts that I think toward you, saith the LORD, thoughts of peace, and not of evil, to give you an expected end."* (Jer 29:11)

I am always amazed at how we can pluck a snippet of Scripture out of a passage and completely ignore the surrounding context to reinforce the consolations we long for. How many times have we heard this scripture in reference to the blessings that God has in store for us? We strain our ears to listen to the wonderful things we yearn to hear and applaud the teachers we have heaped up to soothe our itching ears. Oh, how wonderful are the messages of peace that our prophets have consoled us with!

And yet, the greater context of the scriptures we so glibly quote from often has a much different message than what we wanted to hear. So it is with the above verse from Jeremiah.

Jeremiah was called to prophesy unto Israel in the thirteenth year of Josiah's reign. It was a message of woe and repentance, of judgment to come, and conviction for rebelling against the Lord. Five years later, Josiah discovered the scrolls and instituted a great revival in the land, but Jeremiah continued to bring his message of judgment and repentance.

I can imagine the resistance he received from the Jews of the time. Couldn't this old judgmental prophet see how wonderful their churches were? Why did he not understand that they were in a time of revival? Surely his dark message of repentance no longer applied to them, but this caustic old prophet just wouldn't let go of his old ways. He must not be of God because, praise the Lord, we're all saved and praising the Lord now. There's no need to repent.

The Lord has taken me through the first 25 chapters of Jeremiah over and over. He won't let me leave. Each time I go over them, I see more clearly an overlay of a picture of America and her modern churches. I hear the same cry from God for repentance, but instead of hearing cries of repentance from us, I hear the same words of peace and prosperity that Jeremiah heard from the false prophets of his day.

As the chapters in Jeremiah progress, there is an increased call from God to repent until there finally comes the point when it is too late (Jer. 7:16). And still, issuing from the mouths of the false prophets and priests of the time is a flood of prophecies of peace and prosperity: 'God will never forsake His people, but will return and establish them.' 'Surely God will bless us as we practice our religious ways.' 'God is Love, and He would never send destruction upon us.'

Today's prophets tell us the same messages. And yes, the message of repentance does carry with it the promise of restoration ... _if_ we repent. But just as the people of God in Jeremiah's time could not see the need to repent, even so, our modern churches emphasize praise and worship and turn away from the harder messages of repentance. We will even pluck scriptures as cameo examples of proof that judgment will not come upon us.

But it will come. And though God may deal with us long and plead with us repeatedly -- and yes, even promise us blessings if we will just hearken to His warnings – nevertheless, judgment is determined upon this land for our refusal to acknowledge our departure from the ways of holiness and the fear of God. As Leonard Ravenhill once said, we have more of Hollywood than holiness in our churches.

And the great stone wheel of judgment continues to roll.

The blood of 50 million innocents cries out of the ground of their murder for the sake of adulterous convenience.

One denomination after another has decreed that the abomination of homosexuality is righteous, while our government has decreed that the demonstration of anything godly is against the law.

The translations of God's Word have devolved into paraphrases of the Scriptures but God says we are supposed to tremble at His Word.

The Spirit of God doesn't flow in our services anymore.

There is a complete absence of miracles.

Our altars are empty.

We sing, and we dance, but we do not travail in prayer.

As Amos says, we lie upon beds of ivory, but our hearts are not grieved for the affliction of the lost.

Our hearts are not cut for these things, neither do we acknowledge our sin, but instead look to our prophets for messages of peace, love, blessings, and prosperity. We do not believe that God will send destruction upon us, for we are like the woman with a whore's forehead – we refuse to be ashamed. (Jer. 3:3) We wipe our lips and say, "I have done no wickedness." (Prov. 30:20) "... No man repented him of his wickedness, saying, What have I done?" (Jer. 8:6)

Judgment is determined upon America. Destruction is coming that will be far greater than 9/11 or Katrina. Your prophets have told you that God will spare us and send revival, but it will not come without broken-hearted repentance. The question is, will we repent? Or will we cross the same line that Israel crossed in Jeremiah where it is too late, and God will no longer listen? (Jer. 7:16) Will we not wake up to our spiritual leprosy until we are carried away to Babylon?

Or will we wake up at all?

"The harvest is past, the summer is ended, and we are not saved."
(Jer 8:20)

Psalm 91

> *"He that dwelleth in the secret place of the most High shall abide under the shadow of the Almighty." (Psalms 91:1)*

Psalm 91 is one of the most popular passages in the Bible. We in the church quote it without restraint in many situations. We plug it into the songs we sing, and we look to it for the hope of protection when things go badly. In short, we love the promises and hope it provides us.

A problem arises, however, when we skip over the first verse.

While we hang onto all the promises afforded us throughout the rest of the Psalm, we tend to overlook the conditions placed upon us by verse 1 to initiate those promises. All those promises are true IF we dwell in that secret place of the Most High. The promises of the rest of the Psalm are predicated on the conditions put forth to us in verse 1.

Modern Christianity has proffered a panorama of wonderful blessings but has failed to acknowledge the price that must be paid to receive those blessings. It always sounds so good when we hear of all the blessings that will happen to us, but we shrink from what it will cost us. We want to hear about love, but not about the fear of the Lord. We want to hear what we can get, not what we must do. We love being served but overlook that we are called to serve. We emphasize faith and love but skirt around righteousness and the fear of the Lord.

"Oh yes," they say, "you must be a Christian to receive these blessings, but God does not want us to suffer or be poor." Excuse me? While that sounds so good, and crowds will flock to a message like that, it is not borne out by Scripture. To be blessed is wonderful, but we are also called to the sufferings of the Body of Christ (2 Cor 4:10-12; Phil 3:10) and admonished to deny ourselves and pick up our cross (Luke 9:23). It would be difficult to convince the heroes in Hebrews 11 of this "Pollyanna" gospel. The persecuted Church stands on a shore of sufferings while they watch us sail away on the Good Ship Lollipop.

An old saying among con artists has always been that if you tell people what they want to hear, they will follow you wherever you lead. This has never been truer than with the modern "love" Gospel that has been poured upon us through TV, radio, and our pulpits.

And how do we determine if we are to be included in those wonderful promises of Psalm 91? Why, simply believe in Jesus, of course! We just love God!

Um, it's not quite that simple. There is a difference between Faith and Presumption. Those of us who understand the Word of God in its wholeness know that there are conditions to every promise. These are not conditions that are to be disregarded. No one would believe that they can buy something without paying for it.

"If it is too good to believe," we often say," it isn't true."

"You can't get something for nothing."

"There's nothing free in Life."

And yet, multitudes flock to preachers that will promise us those same empty deals.

I like to say that God is a Jewish businessman — He makes deals. If we want what He has to offer us, there is a price to pay for it. While Salvation may be free to us, nevertheless, someone else paid the price for it. It just wasn't us. Everything has a price.

If we rely upon the blessings and ignore the conditions, we encourage a welfare mentality that weakens the resolve of the people of God to enter into that place of righteousness before God. Half a message results in an anemic Church that falls short of the principles of Faith and thereby encourages a Gospel without power. There is a difference between faith and presumption.

And what happens when the results do not match the empty promises? What happens when God, who must honor His Word, does not respond the way we presumed? What happens when the nice-sounding presumptions we have based our faith on are pulled out from under our feet? What do we have to base our faith on then?

Faith is the substance of things hoped for (Hebrews 11:1), and that substance is what we grasp when we reach through the Door of righteousness to grab hold of the hem of His garment. That Door cannot be opened without the works that accompany true faith. If you want God to do what He says <u>He</u> will do, then you have to do what He says for <u>you</u> to do. And if not, the deal is broken.

Grace is not to be cheapened with empty promises. While it is freely offered to us, it is not maintained without a price. There are conditions. When we ignore those conditions, we set up the people of God for a fall and produce a Church without the power to overcome the tribulations that are upon us.

The Wharf

During a prayer meeting for revival one night, the Lord showed me something so disturbing that I hesitated to share it with the others there. We had gathered together in a home with a sincere desire to pray for revival in our area, but I noticed that the prayers only seemed to be directed to each other, their pastors, their churches, and Christianity in general. No one had even mentioned the lost and the unsaved – they were only praying for themselves and their churches. While I sat there, the Lord showed me this vision:

I saw a large wharf. It was long and wide and stretched out a good distance over the ocean and was filled with a crowd of people up and down its length. It was a bright and sunny day, and I remember feeling how pleasant the weather was. What a wonderful day for a stroll along the pier in your Sunday's finest, meeting and greeting all your friends!

As I looked closer, I realized that these were all Christians. You could see in their bright and smiling faces the joy of salvation and how much they enjoyed being there on that wharf with everyone else. They would gather in little clumps and pray with each other, raising hands and proclaiming blessings upon everyone. Several would drift from group to group, edifying others and speaking a prophetic word of faith into each other's lives. Often I would hear groups lift up praises to God, glorifying His name. Others would be praying for a greater passion to serve Him and a deeper sense of holiness. Still others would be praying for their pastors, their churches, and anyone else they could think of that needed prayer.

In all cases, I noticed that everyone was happy, good-looking, and well dressed. What a wonderful time everyone was having in the Lord! It seemed to be part of their Christian persona, almost as if it identified them as Christians. That made sense to me because of the transforming difference that salvation has upon those who get saved. I've seen hardened faces melt at the altar during Sinner's Prayers every night for years, and I can tell you that the difference that a born-again experience makes on someone affects more than their soul – you can see it all over them. These people on the wharf had that same appearance of joy and peace that only Salvation brings.

As I looked around at the ocean, however, I could see that the sea had a very different look to it than the wharf. The sea was the color of a gun-metal grey and dark blues and looked very cold and dismal. The waves were choppy, tumultuous, and tempestuous. What a different picture this was from what I had seen on the wharf! One was bathed in a warm glow of bright sunshine while the other was overcast in a chilly shadow. The contrast was so stark that it seemed as this sharp difference was portrayed to be that way on purpose.

As I looked out into the sea, I could see masses of people drowning, crying out for help. Their cries would often be choked as another wave splashed over them, and then they would pop up again, waving their hands and crying to the people on the wharf to help them. It was a desperate scene. Masses of people were in the sea, scrambling over each other in a desperate attempt to escape drowning. I could hear the voices screaming as they mingled together into a chorus of misery and desperation.

But no one on the wharf paid any attention.

I was shocked. These were real Christians -- I could tell they were. They not only looked like Christians, but I could also hear them praying over each other, praising God, and admonishing one another to a walk of godliness. But why didn't they help these drowning people? Why didn't they stop praying and throw out some lifelines or, better yet, dive into the water and pull them to safety? Why didn't they do <u>something</u>? Why were they just completely ignoring these desperate cries for help?

And then I realized why. It wasn't because they didn't want to or didn't care. They cared; they just couldn't <u>hear</u> them.

Their ears were stopped up and full of church.

The Furnace Room

"Hast thou commanded the morning since thy days; and caused the dayspring to know his place; That it might take hold of the ends of the earth, that the wicked might be shaken out of it?" (Job 38:12-13)

Revivals have to be prayed in. I think just about everyone agrees with that; I just don't think most people comprehend what that really means.

It has been said that Charles Spurgeon was one of the greatest revival preachers, but he attributed everything to his church. According to David Smithers in an article about Spurgeon, when visitors would come, he would take them to the basement of his church and show them the people on their knees contending before God for souls and declare that this was the powerhouse of the church. "In Spurgeon's eyes," he wrote, "the prayer meeting was the most important meeting of the week." It was this furnace room, not his preaching, that brought the great moves of God that came through him.

Search through revival history, and you will find the same intense reliance on prayer for any move of God. Prior to any serious revival or move of God, people will be crying out to God, sometimes for years before the heavens break wide open. This is the labor room of travail for the Bride of Christ to give birth to revival. Only this kind of intense passion, tears, and travail will move God into a ferocious outpouring of the Holy Spirit.

The Book of Joel, which has God's blueprint for revival, cries to us to bring the entire church into the prayer meeting – including the babies – and cry out to God all night long until He answers. This is what God has laid out for us to do if we want revival. There are no shortcuts, no special circumstances, and no alternate methods.

Okay, so we all know this. We've all heard it a thousand times. Yup, we need to pray. Yup, yup, yup. So when are we going to do it? Excuse me, but if we know this is correct, what will it take for us to crank up the fire? How do we stir up the hearts of the Church to rise up in faith, expectation, and zeal to charge into the prayer room and tear down every principality that stands in the way and shake the Throne of God for the supernatural?

Good question. I wish I had a good answer. If people are not genuinely charged up in the Holy Spirit, their guilty feelings and manufactured zeal will only take them so far. They know they should do this, but their hearts are dragging far behind. As I have said before, water seeks its own level, and it won't take long before people settle back down to their "comfort spot." How do we raise the level of that water and crank up the fire in people's hearts?

I asked the Lord that question. His answer was simple. You want to raise the level of the water? Add more water. Hmmmm.

Throughout the Bible, water is symbolic of the Word of God. The point is simple. We can't turn ourselves into instant prayer warriors through our own efforts. Go ahead. Try it. Pray for 3 hours a day in a strong, loud, contending voice like Elijah did. Let me know how far you get. Only God can give you the power to pray like that. And where does that power come from? The Word. Prayer without faith is pointless, and faith comes by hearing and hearing by the Word of God (Romans 10:17).

This is not exactly a slam dunk, and there is not enough space here to go into a long dissertation on the mechanics of the formulation of revival, but suffice it to say that devouring the Word of God is a good place to start. Without me, Jesus said, you can do nothing (John 15:5) … and He WAS the Word of God.

The rest depends on those faithful few who in receiving their power and faith from the Word of God, know how to contend in prayer and have been battle-trained in storming the Throne of God. This is not for the polite silent prayers of well-meaning church people who clasp their hands and silently offer their thoughts, but for those outrageous souls who will stop at nothing to make their voices heard from on High. This is war, not a skirmish, and the price for failure is not death but eternal torment for countless millions of souls if you do not succeed.

When we look at the great revival preachers that God has used in the past, let us not make the mistake of thinking that they were the ones responsible for the revivals that God brought through them. No, it came through the desperate prayers of some few dedicated, faithful saints who refused to accept defeat but claimed, fought, and won the victory with broken hearts, tear-laden cries, and bended knees in that prayer room and who hung on to the horns of the altar until God moved.

If you want revival, somebody has to get down on their knees.

Snow

It's snowing in Texas.

There is a beautiful softness to the landscape as tender flakes slowly cover the ground in a muted blanket. All seems well with the world.

The kids are excited because they're hoping to get out of school. New Englanders wouldn't be quite so thrilled because they have to shovel it, but here in Texas, we don't have that problem. We can sit back and enjoy the beautiful scene that is laid down before us.

It struck me that before the Flood, it had never rained, nor had it snowed either. The rain that did come was a direct result of the judgment of God upon a world that had grown increasingly wicked. Even though the lessons from the Garden of Eden had not been that long ago, the echoes of God's righteousness had all but faded, and the ears of that generation had turned deaf to the warnings of Noah's preaching. They chose the gratification of flesh rather than the righteousness of God and reaped the severity of His wrath.

And yet, in judgment, we still see the beauty of God. Who can deny the perfection of a snowflake or the beauty of a snow-covered landscape? Over the ages, paintings and poems have tried to describe its ethereal beauty but fall short of what God has freely given us.

It makes me wonder about the personality of God. The Bible describes His righteousness in stark and sometimes frightening terms, but it also gives us a glimpse at a love whose depth is unfathomable. How inadequate is the mind of Man to grasp what God is really like! How can we understand the contrast between His love and judgment that emanate from His incomprehensible holiness?

Psalms 19:1 tells us that the heavens declare the glory of God, and the firmament shows His handiwork, and when I look into the evening sky, I am overwhelmed by the vastness of His intelligence and creation. As David so aptly wrote, "What is man that Thou art mindful of him?"

Only in Eternity will we begin to be able to grasp His glory.

But for now, it is snowing outside. The yard and porch are covered with a cushion of snow, and the trees are all wearing a slender sleeve of white on their dark branches. The air is filled with softly descending snowflakes giving the scene a wonderful feeling of peace. I marvel at how in judgment He has placed such beauty.

I see a glimpse of Calvary in this contrast.

In God's greatest judgment, He has shown us His greatest love.

Curtain of Night

Sometimes I just sit on the porch at night and stare at the black drapery spread across a sky studded with stars that they tell me are so far away that my mind cannot grasp it. I sit there wondering about what lies beyond life, out past the curtain of night and into the realms we will soon pass into. I know that all the things I believe are true, not just because I hope they are, but because they have proven themselves repeatedly through the years.

It's like living in a home with two large rooms – one is your standard living room where you spend most of your time, and the other is a large room where God lives. You can go in there anytime you want by opening the Door and walking in. God is right there. His presence is not something you imagine but something you can tangibly feel. You've had several experiences in there with Him and have actually heard Him speak to you, if not audibly, at least in a very supernatural way.

And yet, when one of your friends who doubts God's existence comes over, try as you might, you cannot convince them of His presence right on the other side of that door. They can argue all they want and quote all sorts of intelligent-sounding theories, some even based on some sophisticated science that you can't understand, but they refuse to cross the threshold of that door to see for themselves. You know that all their fancy, sophisticated ideas would vanish if they could just see for themselves, but it's as if they won't do it because they don't want God to be there.

Silly. If He is there, you'd think they'd want to know.

But instead, they hammer at your faith, dismissing it as old-fashioned, unrealistic, and dumb. But you've been inside that room, and you have met God yourself. He is really there. It doesn't matter what anyone says, you have been in His presence, and nothing can take that away.

I have come to realize that not everybody wants to be saved. Even if they know it is the truth, they will find some kind of way to get around it because they love sin more than righteousness. One day very soon, however, God will cast off the covering that over all the Earth, and we shall see Him as He is (Isaiah 25:7), high and mighty and lifted up above all Eternity. There will be no debate then, no questions or doubts, no mocking and scoffing – just the utter stark realization that, O my God, it's really true!

In the meantime, I labor over how to bring unbelievers to a place where they would be at least willing to step inside that room and see for themselves. Of course, the problem is that to do that, they have to go through that Door, and that is what holds them back more than anything else. You see, it is easy to believe or not believe – it's repentance from sin and a commitment to righteousness that is the great hurdle that most people are not willing to get over. And consequently, that is the ultimate test.

We will not be tried at Judgment on what we believed, what we knew, or what we called ourselves – we will be judged according to our willingness to throw ourselves at His feet, discard our old garment of sin, and step into the Spirit of God so we can be immersed in His righteousness.

It's just like a marriage. You can sign the papers at the Court House, but marriage doesn't mean much if you are not in love with your spouse. If all you did was get married so you could clean the house, make the beds, and cook breakfast, then you missed the whole point. So it is with our marriage to our Bridegroom. If our Christianity is casual and superficial, if our relationship is limited to our attendance at church on Sunday morning, if the real focus of our lives is something other than seeking the Face of God, and if our Christianity is paper-thin, then our salvation is a sham.

If you don't understand what I mean now, you will on the Day of Judgment. On the other side of the black curtain of night is a whole round of angels, a multitude of saints, and the God that created them all. How little we know. But soon – very soon – it shall all be ripped away, and we shall see Him as He is. Then Eternity will seem as normal as day. It will be this life that we went through that will seem like a dream.

Wedding Feast

> *"To an inheritance incorruptible, and undefiled, and that fadeth not away, reserved in heaven for you."* 1st Peter 1:4

You've just entered the Great Hall and are being ushered to your place at the table. The tablecloth stretches from one end to the other in sparkling white linen so pure and white that it is luminous. The place settings are laid out perfectly with rich china plates that seem to glow. The cups and saucers are of a delicate porcelain that seems almost translucent and light to the touch. And the golden jewel-studded goblets that are placed beside each setting stand at attention at each place with a richness that you have never seen. And oh, the silverware! Bowls full of delicious-looking fruits are set all the way down the table, bursting with flavors and scents that call you to reach out and taste them.

As the crowd begins to enter the room and take their places, there is an unspeakable joy of celebration that fills the atmosphere. The rustle of pure white linen can be heard as each person is led to his or her place, where their name is written in pure golden foil on a sheer white vellum card. You can hardly believe you are really here as an angel brings you to your own seat. You are filled with anticipation of the celebration that is to begin.

This is the Marriage Supper of the Lamb, and your reservation has been waiting for you.

As we all settle into our seats, there is a hush that sweeps into the room, and we all stand as the Lamb of God, our Savior who has written our invitation in His own blood, enters the room.

This is the moment we have all been waiting for. This is what has made it all worthwhile. Gone are all the tears, the hardships, and the struggles that brought us here. We have won the victory through the Blood of Jesus and have made our garments white in His Blood and have been found worthy to become His Bride and take part in this final feast of rejoicing.

How handsome is the Bridegroom! How He looks at each of us with a personal intimacy that floods our souls with His overwhelming love for us. We are His forever. We are His Bride, and nothing will ever separate us from Him for Eternity.

This is an event that will take place in the not-too-distant future. Those who have overcome the world will really be there and will enjoy the fruits of this great celebration. Our time on Earth which seems so relevant now will be but a faded memory in the face of the glory of God and the wonders of Heaven. It does not seem so right now, but when it finally comes, it will completely eclipse everything we have experienced in this life.

I would not miss this for anything this world has to offer. I will be there whatever it takes, whatever price that must be paid, whatever tribulations I must endure, whatever battles must be fought. I will be there.

> *"To him that overcometh will I give to eat of the tree of life, which is in the midst of the paradise of God." Revelations 2:7*

Royal Falcons

> *Let thine ear now be attentive, and thine eyes open, that thou mayest hear the prayer of thy servant, which I pray before thee now, day and night, for the children of Israel thy servants, and confess the sins of the children of Israel, which we have sinned against thee: both I and my father's house have sinned. (Nehemiah 1:6)*

I still remember the name of the gang – the Royal Falcons. We were just kids, young punks on the streets of New Jersey, but we thought we were cool – tough guys like the Mafia. Don't mess with us 'cause we're the Royal Falcons!

There were gangs in some of the other neighborhoods that we had to deal with, however, and they thought they were just as bad as we thought we were. Depending on which side of town you were in, you had Blacks, Puerto Ricans, Italians, and the Jewish kids. If you walked into any of those other neighborhoods, it was war; if they walked into yours, they were fair game. Except for the Jewish kids. They were an easy target, so everyone picked on them. But it was always Us against Them, with Us being the good guys, of course.

I am finding the same thing in our religious landscape today. I am bombarded with prophetic words from the latest would-be Elijah about how God is going to send down judgment on America because we are the Great Whore of Babylon or we are just plain bad. Especially the churches. Let's face it, they are the biggest and easiest target, so everybody picks on them.

Honestly, I am beginning to think everybody just wants to spout off so they can feel like they are a prophet with a word from God to point the way. It must feel good because there sure are a lot of them rising up to save the rest of us.

I notice, however, that those who are bringing forth the pronouncements are always the good guys. It's everybody else who are the bad guys.

I don't see it that way. We <u>are</u> "everybody else." It's not someone else's fault – it's ours. It's not a matter of we're the good guys because we can see clearly what the problem with America is. No, we're the bad guys because we can see clearly what the problem with America is, and instead of leading the way to fix it, we just point at everybody else.

The only way to revival and restoration with God is through repentance.

Okay, so who's going to start? Is it going to be the crazy Pentecostals? The emotionless Baptists? The plastic Evangelicals? The idolatrous Catholics? The obsolete Methodists? Or the liturgical Episcopalians? Who? Who is going to start the ball rolling?

How about me? Why not start with me? After all, judgment will begin at the house of God, won't it? Maybe it's not somebody else, but it is me that needs to come to a place of repentance before God and ask Him to please forgive me. Maybe it's my fault, not somebody else's. Maybe instead of pointing at someone else's need to repent, I should lead the way.

After all, that's what Nehemiah and Daniel did.

> *"O Lord, to us belongeth confusion of face, to our kings, to our princes, and to our fathers, because we have sinned against thee." (Daniel 9:8)*

Best Sellers

"Study to show thyself approved unto God, a workman that needeth not to be ashamed, rightly dividing the word of truth. But shun profane and vain babblings for they will increase unto more ungodliness. And their word will eat as doth a canker of who is Hymenaeous and Philetus; who concerning the truth have erred, saying that the resurrection is past already; and overthrow the faith of some." 2 Timothy 15-19

Wait a minute. Let me get this straight. You mean that the Apostle Paul showed up preaching a revolutionary new doctrine that you can have salvation by believing that God sent His own Son to die for your sins, raised Him from the dead, and that through simple repentance and belief, you can be transformed, heart and soul. This was not from a theological bent like you heard in the synagogue or the church, but this was with a power and an anointing that caused faith to burst forth in your heart. You were completely transformed and regenerated by this, and it changed the entire outlook of your life. You were saved, born-again, and free for the first time in your life. You don't know how this has happened; you just know that it has!

Ah, but now you've got a better idea. Yeah, the Apostle Paul was great in bringing this Gospel to you, but you have risen above his arcane ideas, and now you have a new and better revelation in God. Feeling pretty good about yourself, are you?

As amazing and stupid as this may seem, it is an old and continuing pattern. And Paul warns Timothy to dive into the Word because it is the only defense against these profane babblings. The more you veer away from studying the Word, the greater tendency you will have to be enamored with fascinating theories that range from new perspectives on foundational doctrines to wild conspiracy theories about end-time prophecy. Neat stuff. It just doesn't produce faith.

Profane doesn't necessarily mean bad – it just means worldly. It's not that it is ungodly; it's just not godly. But it sure can be fascinating! And the allure is the same that drew Eve to the Tree of the Knowledge of Good and Evil – a fruit desired to make one wise. It doesn't make you wise; it just creates a carnal desire for wisdom. It generates a "form of godliness" but denies "the power thereof"(2 Tim 3:5). They are clouds without rain and wells without water (2 Pet. 2:17). It gets you to keep reaching, but you are "never able to come to the knowledge of the truth" (2 Tim 3:7).

Studying the Word is not an admonition to absorb a textbook knowledge about God. It is to feed your soul with the Bread of Life because it is the only defense against the canker of religious fables and the profane and vain babblings of carnal theological scholasticism. The object is not to train your mind to know stuff; it is to engraft the Word into your heart so that it can bring forth life.

It never ceases to amaze me how many people that I run into who claim to be Christians – some even assuming leadership roles of deacons, pastors, bishops, even apostles and prophets – but are unfamiliar with the depths of the Word of God upon which their authority is supposed to be based. But ask them about any of the latest Christian best-sellers, spiritual fads, or cute new ideas, and they can tell you all about them. They can spout off all sorts of colloquial scriptures they've heard about, but they have so little depth in the Bible that they have no idea where they are found nor the context within which they were written. No wonder the modern church is so anemic!

When we forsake the source of all power and wisdom in order to lend ourselves to easier and more "modern" Pied Pipers that are more to our liking, we abdicate our rights to go directly to the Throne of God for our sustenance. The veil of carnal-mindedness that we draw across our hearts blinds us to the call for severe righteousness, making it seem too harsh and blinding. The subtle hues of compromise are much more comfortable and woo us into shades of grey and shadows of apostasy. "Preach unto us smooth things," they cry unto Isaiah, "prophesy unto us deceits…" (Isaiah 30:10)

Paul adds the warning:

"For the time will come when they will not endure sound doctrine; but after their own lusts shall they heap to themselves teachers, having itching ears." (2 Tim 4:3)

Perhaps next, we will see a new best-selling Christian self-help book written by Stephen King. Now that should be entertaining!

Thermometer for the Church

> *"Any objection to the carryings on of our present gold-calf Christianity is met with the triumphant reply, 'But we are winning them!' And winning them to what? To true discipleship? To cross-carrying? To self-denial? To separation from the world? To crucifixion of the flesh? To holy living? To nobility of character? To a despising of the world's treasures? To hard self-discipline? To love for God? To total committal to Christ? Of course, the answer to all these questions is no." - A.W.Tozer*

> *"And I, brethren, if I yet preach circumcision, why do I yet suffer persecution? Then is the offence of the cross ceased ... But God forbid that I should glory, save in the cross of our Lord Jesus Christ, by whom the world is crucified unto me, and I unto the world." (Galatiens 5:11 & Gal 6:14)*

Good intentions alone do not equate to good results.

Over the years, I have watched churches with good intentions subscribe to a myriad of programs, seminars, study courses, video presentations, and vaudeville productions in an attempt to launch their church into an exciting, new and vibrant walk with God – something that will energize their congregation and enliven their pastor so that his normally dull sermons will be revitalized with power and excitement. And it sometimes works ... for a week or two. But water seeks its own level and will always sink back to where it is the most comfortable.

God did not leave us without His instructions; the blueprint for a true revival is in the Book of Joel. The problem is that that solution is not what we want to hear. And since we are so smart, sophisticated, and educated, we will figure out our own solution; thank you very much. As a result, we are left running around in circles trying desperately to catch our tails.

What is it that we really want? Are we really after revival? Or do we just want a richer experience so that we can be spiritually entertained?

The thermometer for the church is not the Sunday service which we all consider to be the apex of our spiritual week, but the Wednesday night prayer meeting. (Did you even know you had a prayer meeting on Wednesday?) There is where you will find the furnace for the entire church. It is the Labor Room where the moves of God are birthed. If there is no fire there, you won't find it anywhere else. The price for real revival is not paid by the front office, in the offering basket, community projects, or with mindless accolades and "Ataboys" for the preacher. It is paid on your knees.

If that is so, then why aren't our Wednesday night prayer meetings packed to capacity? Why are they so dull that no one wants to come? Could it be that we really don't believe that God will answer our prayers? Or maybe our prayers are so anemic that He doesn't even hear us? Or perhaps we just really don't care that much? Life is good; we're okay. Hope everybody has a nice day.

Revivals must be prayed in with deep, contending, gate-crushing, desperate prayer. It has been said that God doesn't answer prayer – He answers desperate prayer! Desperate prayer like Rachael's Cry in Genesis 30:1 - "Give me souls or else I will die!" How bad do you have to want it? Bad enough to die.

If you want God to send the rain, then you will have to pray like Elijah - you have to storm the Throne of God. Prayer moves God. If you want God to move, then you have to contend before Him until He does.

Revival has a price, and it is not the price that human flesh would like to pay. But if we will shed the baggage of our own theological endeavors and instead allow God to strip us down to the bare metal of our souls so that our only sufficiency is in Him, then we will find not only the strength, but the will and inspiration to walk that crucified walk that leads to the Cross.

And only there will the fire begin to burn.

Sound Speech

> *"In all things showing thyself a pattern of good works: in doctrine showing incorruptness, gravity, sincerity, sound speech, that cannot be condemned; that he that is of the contrary part may be ashamed, having no evil thing to say of you."* Titus 2:7,8

I used to think that sound speech meant not saying any curse words. And be careful how you use "hell" and "damn." I suppose that is still true, but looking deeper into the Greek, I see that there is much more to this little, obscure phrase of "sound speech" than just tiptoeing around raw colloquialisms. There is something here that smacks of a stiff reproof to our idea of sophisticated preaching today.

The word "speech" comes from the Greek *"logos."* – the Word. Jesus was the *"Logos."* Literally, it is intelligent speech, but it is also given the added emphasis as the intelligent speech that comes from the mouth of God. As God's ambassadors on Earth, our speech should reflect that same divine Logos.

Paul's intent in the book of Titus was not to create good citizens with pleasant manners but to defend the Faith by instructing us how to maintain our testimony before the unsaved. It is not a matter of saying nice things so no one will get mad at you, but having the type of speech (or logos) that will make them ashamed of themselves for bringing any accusation against you and the church. This is war, not etiquette!

It is here that the word Paul uses for "sound" plays such an important role. The Greek word is *"hugies"* (or *"hugros,"* depending on how you spell it), which means "moist." It is translated as "sound" or "healthy," such as a healthy body would be moist.

But there is another to look at this. The Word of God is repeatedly pictured as water. We see it in Ephesians 5:26 as the washing of the water of the Word. It is used again in the story of Cana of Galilee as a lesson to fill ourselves as waterpots of earthen stone to the brim with the water of the Word so that it may turn into the wine of the Spirit. That symbolism of water as the Word of God is seen in many other places throughout both the Old and New Testaments.

If our speech is to be moist with the water of the Word of God – saturated, let's say – then the rest of that verse begins to make a lot more sense. We will always be attacked and accused by the enemy, no matter what we say or do, but when we stand up in the power of the Holy Spirit and our speech is saturated with the Word of God, we deliver a powerful testimony to the unbelievers, not in the wisdom of words (as Paul writes in 1 Corinthians 2:4) but in demonstration of the Spirit and power. What an incredible difference that is!

Sophisticated speech, good manners, and theologically intelligent sermons will not win the souls nor convince the gainsayers. Only the power of God through the Blood of Jesus Christ can do that. Even speech that is laced with Bible scriptures cannot do that unless it is delivered in the Spirit and not in the letter. In other words, the water cannot be artificial – it has to come from the Throne of God. Theological scholasticism and carnal religion cannot duplicate the power that only flows through the water from the true Logos. Anything less than that is just another attempt to build our own Tower of Babel, which will ultimately fall.

Theological sermons that sound more like a college lecture than Holy Ghost preaching foster debate, not faith. Only when we allow our logos to be saturated with God's Logos will we bring forth a testimony of power that will shame those who are contrary to us and shut their mouths.

Saturate yourselves in the Word. Fill your waterpot to the brim. Look deeply into its reflection to cleanse the well of your heart. Let the sap from the True Vine flow through you so that it and not your carnal effort will bring forth fruit. Throw away your prepared messages of carnal preaching and stand in the power of God to deliver your sermons. Let the water of Life flow freely through you, not the dead, dried-out dust of religious boredom. Preach in faith, not in theology.

Shut up and let God speak.

Sorcery

> *" (As it is written, I have made thee a father of many nations,) before him whom he believed, even God, who quickeneth the dead, and calleth those things which be not as though they were.*
>
> *Who against hope believed in hope, that he might become the father of many nations, according to that which was spoken, So shall thy seed be. "* Romans 4:16-18

What an incredible statement of faith! To believe not only the unseen but also the incomprehensible simply because God said so! Abraham believed God! But how is it that we so readily try to take this great pronouncement of faith in God's creative power and ascribe it to ourselves?

Abraham had just settled in Haran with his brother and family when God told him to pack up and leave. Just when everything was going so well! Just go, God told him, and He would tell him where he was going when he got there.

So Abraham went.

Then God declares unto Abraham great promises that he would inherit the land, that all nations would be blessed because of him, and that his seed would be like the dust of the world. Pretty astounding stuff for a simple sheepherder to hear.

Abraham wasn't sure where all this was going, but he knew it was true. After all, this didn't come from Abraham's imagination but directly from the mouth of God. Abraham was even visited by the priest of the Most High God, Melchizedek, and was blessed again. Okay, now he knows that this is no coincidence, but this is real. But what exactly is going on?

And then, one more time, God appears to him and promises His all-encompassing protection and reward. Pretty heavy stuff for anyone, even someone as righteous as Abraham. But what is Abraham supposed to do with all this? What is the purpose of all these great and precious promises? He has no children, so who will he pass this on to after he dies? What is the point?

God then promises Abraham that his seed would be like the stars in the sky. And Abraham believes Him. He believed God because He was God. God could quicken Abraham's sexually dead body to bring life out of a dead womb. Or as the King James Version puts it, "calleth those things which be not as though they were." Abraham did not have to know how God did it or why. He didn't even have to believe that God <u>could</u> do it – He simply believed that He <u>would</u>. And God counted that to him for righteousness.

But what do I hear in the churches today? "Oh, praise the Lord, brother. Just speak the word and call those things which be not into existence!" "Just name it and claim it!" "Call it into being!" Yeah, right, just snap your fingers and speak it into the wind, and all kinds of stuff will pop into existence!

Excuse me, but where did we get this kind of outrageous audacity from? Who gave you the power of creation? Do you really think that because you got saved that you automatically inherited the divine powers of creation? Do you think you can just snap your fingers and speak something into existence? That is not faith – that is sorcery.

The Bible says that the kingdom of God is not in word but in power. In other words, we have power in God through our faith and our broken submission to Him, but our faith is in God's power, not our own. Magic words do not possess a power of their own. To attribute magical power to words that we speak is not faith. It is sorcery, and it is sin. It's the kind of stuff you learn at Hogwarts with Harry Potter.

The funny thing is that I hear Christians misquote Romans 4:17 all the time, attributing God's divine power to themselves, but it always seems to come from Christians who have not found that broken, crucified walk in God. These are the same Christians who are enamored with prosperity, blessings, and wealth and believe there will be a great transference of wealth from the sinners to themselves.

Their main focus seems to be not on what they can do for God but on what God can do for them. They don't want to pay the price that is required, but they sure want to reap the rewards. They don't want to break their spirits or crucify their flesh, but they expect the deeper spiritual walk that only comes from sacrifice. They won't prostrate themselves and cry out upon the altar of repentance with fastings, prayers, and tears, but they want to walk around with a power they neither earned nor deserve.

Everybody wants to be an Elijah, but nobody wants to pay the price.

Abraham believed God and was willing to leave everything behind to follow God into a strange land where he was a stranger. He believed God because if God said it, He would do it. God could bring forth that which did not exist into existence. God had the power, not Abraham. Abraham's power was in that he believed God, not that he became God.

To ascribe to ourselves the divine power of creation that belongs only to God is not the righteousness of faith but the wickedness and pride of Satan, who desired to become like the Most High.

Folly of Fools

"The wisdom of the prudent is to understand his way; but the folly of fools is deceit"
Proverbs 14:8

I heard from a dear sister in the Lord that someone had come to visit her missionary work and had prophesied over her that the Lord is ready to move in her ministry in a mighty way. (sigh) Where have I heard this before?

Maybe it's just my imagination, but it seems these kinds of prophecies are rampant in the Church today and have been for the last 30 years or so. I have heard this same thing over and over, but I'm still waiting to see where and when these great and mighty moves are. I hear it will be in Dallas; oh no, it will be in Omaha; no, Phoenix, no, it's this church; no, that one, etc.

And then there are the personal prophesies of blessings and a great move of God in your life: "Oh, God is about to bring you into your harvest!" (Pronounced with the obligatory affected voice and tremolo.) Oh, to hear that God is paying personal attention to you! And He is going to elevate you to great honor!

Perhaps my attention has drifted off, and I have not been patient enough to wait, but surely, after all these years, <u>something</u> should have burst forth by now for somebody. But I'm still waiting.

I hate to say anything negative because we're all supposed to think positively. (Aren't we? Or is that just some advice from Dale Carnegie?) Nevertheless, the last thing I would want to do is sow doubt into a profession that calls for faith, but it just seems that there is just something missing.

I've noticed that these prophetic blessings come without any conditions or price. It's all just going to fall out of the sky right into our laps. Nothing about repentance or broken-hearted contending in prayer or even seeking the face of God in any depth. Praise the Lord, just sit back and receive it. Boy, it sure sounds good.

There's another thing that I've noticed about these prophecies -- they are always delivered by self-proclaimed prophets who never cross the line to prophesy about judgment. You never hear them talk about repentance. Never. Like roadside Gypsies, it is always about the blessings and promises of prosperity. It's like they are cruising around in a dream, and everything is beautiful. No harsh judgments ever come out of their mouths, only benedictions of blessing, peace, and love ... and, of course, prosperity. They do not speak of the fear of God but have changed that to "respect" and "reverence." A quick read of the Bible should tell you that there is a difference between respect and reverence and the serious fear of God. But they don't see a difference. Their view of the core personality of God is no longer holiness and righteousness, but peace and love.

Human nature has an innate tendency to choose the comfortable over the harsh. Paul said that we heap up teachers to ourselves having itching ears (2 Tim. 4:3). Isaiah puts it well in 30:10, "Speak unto us smooth things; prophesy deceits." And the prophet proclaims that "my people love to have it so" (Jer. 5:31)

But where are the prophets that are like the ones we read about in the Word of God? Maybe they're in the same place that they've always been – pushed aside out of the way.

That is why the folly of fools is deceit. (Prov. 14:8) We are more willing to deceive ourselves into hearing what we <u>want</u> to hear rather than the harsh realities of sacrifice, subjection, and righteousness. Like Pied Pipers, these "prophets of vanity" multiply around us, promising everything our hearts yearn for. It's what we want to hear, so we convince ourselves that it must be true.

But ask these prophets <u>how</u> they heard this word from God, and you will get an answer that is as fuzzy as their predictions. Ethereal whiffs of spiritual feelings are not declarations from God. They're just puffs of wind, breezes of imagination that ride on waves of vanity.

Ask a real prophet of God, and he will tell you that God spoke to him – like speech, as in words, not thoughts. Ah, but we don't believe in that kind of supernatural stuff anymore, do we? We have become oh, so spiritual now that we can depend on our "feelings" to lead us. And, of course, our feelings always seem to lead in the same direction.

There is a simple litmus test for prophets written in the Bible in black and white. Pass the test, and you're for real. Flunk the test, and you are a false prophet. Of all the "prophets of peace" that swarm around us (everyone wants to be "prophetic" these days), I am still waiting to see any of them pass this test:

"The prophet which prophesies of peace, when the word of the prophet shall come to pass, then shall the prophet be known that the Lord hath truly sent him." Jeremiah 28:9

Or, as they say in Jersey, "Put up, or shut up."

"For the idols have spoken vanity, and the diviners have seen a lie, and have told false dreams; they comfort in vain." (Zechariah 10:2)

Leprosy in the House

> *"Then the priest shall command that they empty the house, before the priest go into it to see the plague, that all that is in the house be not made unclean: and afterward the priest shall go in to see the house: "*
> Leviticus 14:36

The laws of leprosy for a house still apply today, especially when uncleanness is found in a house of God.

According to the Law, when leprosy is found in a house, the house has to be emptied of everything in it and then scrubbed and scoured to scrape out every last vestige of the disease. If the plague is stopped, then you can bring everything back in, but if not, then everything – the house, walls, roof, and everything that was still inside it – has to be broken down to rubble and taken outside the city.

When leprosy is found in the house of God, the same rules apply, no matter where the uncleanness is found. If it is found in those in leadership or the congregation, they must be scoured and cleaned. How much more if it is found in the pastor himself! If it is the doctrine, the teachings, the service, or the music, then the house must be cleansed.

Too often, I hear people excuse, justify, and minimize sins found in their church and leadership. They excuse them away with weak responses about how because we are all human and we all sin every day, we shouldn't judge. God loves us all and understands that we are just flesh.

Excuse me? Where did that come from? Geez, doesn't that sound familiar to you? Like maybe in the very beginning? "… Ye shall not surely die." Isn't this the same lie that Satan has been using for the last 6,000 years?

First of all, the Word of God says that He will give us the power to overcome all sin and reinforces that with a command to be perfect as your Father in Heaven is perfect. So, God thinks you can do it, but Satan tells you that you cannot. Whom will you believe?

God <u>does</u> understand our weaknesses. That's why He sent His Son to die for us and deliver us from sin. Grace is not an excuse to continue in sin – it is the power of God to overcome it. To adhere to any other doctrine is to trample the Blood of Jesus and count it as an unholy thing. It is as if you do not believe there is power in the Blood, and so His sacrifice on the Cross was for naught.

And Judgment? How much it is like Satan to try and convince us to sheer away from judgment and to consider it as being something evil! If we do not stand for the righteousness of God, then who will declare Truth to this generation? We are commanded to warn those in sin, not placate them with soothing lies. He never said <u>not</u> to tell them the truth. He commanded us to first get the beam out of our eye and stand in righteousness ourselves. <u>Then</u> we can see clearly to reprove others. This is not condemnation – this is giving life!

God wants His Church clean. He wants a Bride without spot or wrinkle. The Book of Revelations does not say He will give the Tree of Life to those who <u>try</u>. It says He will give it to those who <u>overcome</u>. That's why He tells us to examine ourselves.

Jesus is the High Priest who will examine the house and declare us clean or unclean. Judgment will begin at the house of God. Clean the House; scrub the walls; scour the place inside out; come out from a church that is not clean. If you decide to remain inside a house that has leprosy by making excuses for sin, you also will be carried outside the camp.

Revival does not come without deep, corporate repentance and will never come to the Church as long as there is sin in the house. The trick is in recognizing it and being honest with ourselves and with God. Only when the Church is clean will it ever see a true move of God.

Water in the Desert

For some reason, it seems darkness falls more quickly at the Equator than it does in North America. It is not that late – only an hour or two after sunset – and the only description that comes to mind is the old saying, "Blacker than the insides of a cat's belly." It is so dark that the blackness has a rich, velvety texture -- you can feel the darkness. It makes the display overhead all that much more blazing. The heavens most certainly declare the glory of God – especially way out here in the desert.

We are 50 kilometers from the nearest blacktop road. There are no stores, gas stations, or cell phone service. No TV, newspapers, or electricity … and little water. We are in the bush country of Africa. You would think that the level of sophistication amongst the people who sparsely inhabit this place would be rudimentary, but I have found them to be surprisingly aware, engaged, and intelligent. Like the doctor whose place we are staying at – an Army medical doctor for years who chose to come home to this place to be with his people, the Massai.

We are camping inside his compound. (Actually, I'm sleeping inside the house because I'm too old to sleep on the ground, but the others are out in tents.) There is a barrier of thorned acacia branches that make a prickling 3-foot wall around the compound to keep out predators like lions, leopards, and hyenas. Yeah, nice place, Africa. Great place for the kids to play. But hey, I have been reassured that it's safe. The lions only come down in the rainy season. And the leopards …?

I tell folks that the landscape and arid climate is much like Texas, but that's not exactly true. There is faint wildness to the feel of this place that is distinctively African. Almost like a sandy, raw and wild edge that is felt rather than seen. Perhaps it's from the exotic adventure books that I read as a kid which give this place a certain flavor that is unlike any other place in the world. Imagination or not, it certainly feels different here.

The Massai who are here favor bright reds and yellows in their dress – a sharp contrast to the muted colors of the desert. But while they may be dressed in the bizarre costumes of the Massai, living in small Hobbit-like mud huts and cut off from the world, they do possess a piercing hunger for the things of God. It's as if they have shed the layer of worldliness like you would a layer of clothing and now have a clearer and cleaner exposure to the things that are not of this world.

There is none of the "churchiness" that you find in the churches back home, especially the evangelical churches. This is straight stuff, clear focus, no-frills religion. It strikes me funny that many church people would probably say, "What 'churchiness'?" Well, if they could see it, they wouldn't be in it. These Christians aren't exposed to "Church." What they have is faith, and that's what sustains them in this dry spiritual desert.

I have brought Bibles here – both the written and the talking radio for those who cannot read. It is like showers of rain in the desert to them. You can't describe what it is like to see them get their own Bible – their very own! One that is not ripped and held together with tape and rubber bands! One that is not shared by 30 or so people in the church!

Water in the desert. Yeah, that's a good way to describe it. Water is used in the Bible as an analogy for the Word of God. Not only as a cleansing agent in Ephesians 5:26 and the laver of brass in Exodus, but also as a producer of fruit and a giver of life, a picture of the outpouring of the Spirit of God, and the latter rain.

The drought of this parched desert makes the people here desperate for that water of life, while the worldly lushness of a saturated land like ours is not as thirsty for the same.

Prophetic Spirits

> *"A true witness delivereth souls: but a deceitful witness speaketh lies." (Proverbs 14:25)*

I am worried about a trend I see in today's churches that seems to have caught on without any restraints or even any questioning of its validity. I am talking about our rush toward pursuing this "prophetic spirit" that so many Christians have been enamored with.

Churches these days are rife with schools for prophets, even initiating schools for children to learn how to develop a prophetic spirit. How we long to hear from God! But is this a talent that can be learned or taught? The retort always points to the references to the "schools of prophets" in the books of Samuel and 1st and 2nd Kings. But were these classrooms to teach young people Prophecy 101? Is there a Five-Step program to becoming a prophet? Something that can be written down in a manual for would-be prophets?

The Bible does not mention a school <u>for</u> prophets – it talks of a "company" of prophets. The Hebrew is "hebel," a union or group that is woven together like a rope. It is related to "habel," which has to do with a pledge or a security taken. In other words, there were groups of prophets who were bound together by their commitment to one another and to God. No schools. No course of education. No seminars for 99 bucks to sign up for, and be the first on your block to have a "prophetic spirit." A true prophet of God is called, not schooled – and God calls you, not the other way around.

I have noticed a remarkable telltale sign that is universal with these "prophetic spirits" – they never talk about repentance, judgment, or the fear of God. It is always something warm and fuzzy about how God is going to bless you and how you are about to "enter into your harvest," or something innocuous like that. How nice.

But that's not what I see in the Bible. As a matter of fact, Jeremiah declares that when a prophet of peace utters a word of prophecy, we are to wait and see if it happens first. (Jer. 28:9). According to the

Bible, the effectiveness of a prophet is measured by his ability to bring the people of God to a place of repentance. (Jer. 23:22) Maybe we should read the 23rd chapter of Jeremiah again before we start spouting off with our "fair-haired boy" prophesies. Or is that not in the syllabus for our schools of prophets?

The job of a prophet is to stand in the gaps of the wall that has been broken down and declare unto the people of God their sins and transgressions so that they may repent and come back to God. But those prophets always have a difficult time getting any traction in the Church. They're not polite, nor do they seem to care if they hurt our feelings. Maybe that's because they really <u>have</u> heard from God, not from their ethereal thoughts. They know exactly what the message is and who it is that has told them. It doesn't matter if you don't believe it – you will soon enough. But our prophets today keep their message "positive" and "edifying" so that it always appeals to the crowd with "itching ears."

A solitary prophet, who tried for years to get Israel to repent from their "churchy" ways, sat in a ruined city after everything he had tried to call them to had failed, and cried out,

> *"Thy prophets have seen vain and foolish things for thee: and they have not discovered thine iniquity, to turn away thy captivity; but have seen for thee false burdens and causes of banishment."*
> *(Lamentations 2:14)*

If we find ourselves in the same situation, we can expect the same results.

What we are chasing is not some prophetic spirit from God but a spirit of divination from the powers of darkness. It is designed to lead the Church away from a place of repentance and the fear of God into a "Pollyanna" Gospel where everything is beautiful and all about love. But honestly, they are only telling us what we want to hear. They are the Gypsy tea leaf readers of the church today. And we respond by buying their books and videos as they lead us away like a Pied Piper.

But the reality is much harsher. This is war, and Satan has done his job well in defusing our outlook into one of détente. As we are lulled to sleep and drift off into a kinder and gentler Gospel that leads away from repentance, we lose our sharp edge and our ability to see with a spiritual clarity that only comes through the fear of God. We have forsaken the right way and chosen for ourselves an easier path that leads away from the Cross, not toward it. Jonah gasps to us from the belly of the whale that those who observe lying vanities forsake their own mercy (Jonah 2:8).

Let us take care that the "word from the Lord" we are itching to speak over others is from the Throne of God and not some enticing spirit of divination.

Insanity

During one of the services we had in Uganda, an old woman was healed of insanity while sitting out in the congregation. This happened during the service. No one laid hands on her or prayed over her – the Lord just healed her right then and there.

I remember how excited she was, but the translator couldn't keep up with her excitement when she tried to tell us about it, so I didn't understand what had happened. She went home for the lunch break and was so excited that her daughters thought she had completely flipped. And they thought it was our fault! They tried to keep her from coming back for the afternoon service, but she broke out of the house and came anyway.

I saw her when she came in. She was a bit late, but I didn't think much about it at the time. During that 2nd service, the Lord washed through her again and completed her healing. This time we heard her story and were able to understand what a great deliverance she had had.

Imagine being immersed in a cloud of confusion as if your mind was completely underwater. You can't see straight, you can't think clearly, and your entire perception of life is warped. Your life is spent in mental torment. And then, the Spirit of God washes through you, and you are healed in an instant. You can think again. The fog is blown away, and you can see clearly for the first time in who knows how long! What an incredible life-changing experience! Your world is suddenly filled with light and understanding, and you are free!

My primary passion has been to bring revival to the churches, and the vision set before me has been to break the hold of complacency on them and shatter the glass ceiling that limits their faith. Once those fetters are broken, the church is free to soar into the presence of the Holy Spirit and ignite with the fire of God.

But revival is also personal. How grand is the release of God's mercy on us as individuals! What rejoicing there is when a single person is set free from the misery and burden of sickness, torment, and sin. I notice that Jesus spent more of his time dealing with individuals than with whole synagogues, but we tend to focus more on the corporate body.

We talk about revival in great flowing terms while we attend seminars and conferences in a vain attempt to spawn a revival in our churches. We read books and institute programs that we've been told will work for our church. We invite speakers to energize our congregations, and we promote any prophet who will encourage us that surely revival will come to our church. But Jesus pointed us to that one lost sheep for whom there is more rejoicing than for the 99 that are already in the church. It is for that one individual that He died.

Perhaps that is where we should place our focus. Perhaps instead of trying to legislate revival for the church, we need to change our definition of what revival really is.

For that one old woman in Uganda, it was that singular moment when God delivered her from a life of torment.

Substance

> *"Now faith is the substance of things hoped for, the evidence of things not seen." Hebrews 11:1*

I had an incredible experience last night.

Lately, I have been wondering what makes the gift of healing work. There seems to be something fundamental that I am not understanding. Why does it work sometimes and sometimes not? There are times I can feel the anointing flow through my hands like a stream of oil right into the person I am praying for. Other times it is like an electric current. And just like that, they are healed! And then, sometimes, no matter how hard I pray, nothing happens. I'll even try to imagine it in my head in a vain attempt to make it happen, but when it doesn't work, it just doesn't work. So what am I missing?

I've often felt that if we could just get over to the other side of Eternity to see the reality of the spiritual world and the unreality of the physical world, we would realize just how simple the working of faith really is. The only problem with that is getting back to the physical world to start working with what I learned.

Nevertheless, I'm missing something here, and I have to believe there is a simple answer. I'm just stuck in this world looking through a glass darkly, as Paul wrote, and I just don't get it.

But last night, I got a glimpse of it, and wow, was it powerful! Simple, but so profound that I knew in an instant that it takes a piercingly spiritual revelation to just be able to grasp the simplicity of the answer.

I was at a revival prayer meeting that I go to every week where our focus is mostly for a true Holy Ghost revival for this area. While I am mainly focused on Africa because I firmly believe that the last great revival will start from there, I also feel it is all interconnected. Pray for one, and you'll get the other. Makes sense to me.

As the Spirit of God began to descend on us and the prayers began to get energized, I could feel the level of energy rise in me, and pretty soon, I was praying with ... how do I put this ... a rock-solid strength of conviction? Complete and total faith? Determined assuredness? All I know is that it felt like I was treading on a solid rock of utter faith that was so sure that there was not even a shadow of doubt or wondering. I was approaching the Throne of God with all the holy boldness of a warrior in God. I had rights to the Throne of God that were established on nothing less than the power of the Blood of Jesus Christ, and nothing – NOTHING – could stop me!

This was not a matter of belief. This was fact – a reality that transcended the Universe and beyond. The utter simplicity of it was astounding. It was written. It was the Rock-solid Word of God. It was Eternal Truth. It was beyond my physical being and was the very substance of Eternity.

I began to pray like a sledgehammer hitting an anvil of solid steel. I stood in a holy boldness that would have scared me otherwise. (It probably scared the people in the pew in front of me.) I challenged the Almighty God! I commanded the power of the Holy Spirit! No compromise, no yielding, no retreat. I claimed an answer from God before all the holy angels and the entire arena surrounding the Throne of God. I was not backing down. I absolutely refused to take "no" for an answer.

I had the incredible simplicity of Faith in His Word to demand – yes, demand – for God to move and fulfill His promises to me. I felt like I was smashing through spiritual barriers as if they were spider webs. Nothing could stand in my way as I stood before the Holy of Holies and challenged Almighty God to do what He said He would do.

Man, I was hitting the target hard! Every time I'd slam down my demands, the Holy Spirit would hit me in a burst, and I would start laughing again and again. I was on a roll!

What struck me was that it was so simple. If we could just pierce through the veil of this flesh that clouds our spiritual vision to see the reality of His Word, we would finally grasp the rock-solid assuredness of His promises to us that, yes, we <u>can</u> move mountains by faith, we <u>can</u> raise the dead, we <u>can</u> ask what we will, and He will do it for us. But it takes a piercing of that veil to grab hold of the substance of faith.

I believe that God wants us to pray with holy boldness, but that kind of "warrior praying" has dissipated from our churches over the years. We had this kind of holy boldness once upon a time, but we have lost it to modern Christianity's sophisticated but anemic ways. When God begins to move upon us again, I believe we will once again see real Holy Ghost warriors rise up to meet the challenge and claim the birthright that we have long ago sold for a bowl of porridge.

And then we will see the greatest revival of all time because we were not afraid to stand in blood-washed faith and demand it of God.

Talk is Cheap

" Thus saith the Lord God; woe unto the foolish prophets, that follow their own spirit, and have seen nothing!" Ezekiel 13:3

About now, I'm sure you've had your fill of all the prophecies for this new year. This is going to be the year that God is going to do this and do that, move here and move there. This is the year of your deliverance, of your blessing, of whatever it is that you have been waiting for. This is the year. Hang on; here it comes.

Funny. Weren't those the same things we heard last year? And the year before? Ah, but this is a new year, so we get to hear them all over again. (Sigh) If these were about secular things, we'd call these people con artists. But no, this is in the Church, so we call them prophets.

There is a real danger in these kinds of prophecies of peace. I understand that we all want to encourage the Church to be edified and to strengthen our faith, but is this the word from the Lord, or is it a ploy to bring us into a false sense of security and to weaken our defenses?

According to Ezekiel, false prophets only serve to keep the people of God from repentance by deceiving them into thinking that all is well between them and God. Their message is always the same – God loves you and is going to shower you with all your hopes and dreams. Everything is wonderful. Relax and be raptured.

It would be nice if all we had to do was sit back and watch God do all the work, but that's not how it reads in His Word. Just as Israel broke her covenant with God in becoming worldly, so we have fallen far from the great calling in God that we once had.

Do we still have it? Well, the gifts and calling of God are without repentance, to be sure, but that calling also cries out for us to walk deeply in the Spirit of God to receive it. And we have lost that. We say we do, but look at the on-fire Christians from just a couple of generations ago who prayed and fasted their guts out for lost souls, and you will be sorely embarrassed. No, all we do is talk.

I get tired of reading emails, essays, and mini-messages about how God will send a great move of the Spirit to us and call the Church back to a glorious revival. Sorry, but after a while, it all sounds like just so much white noise. Talk, talk, talk.

Talk is cheap. Even the Bible says so. (Pro 14:23) When are we going to do something besides talk?

No revival comes without repentance -- not only personal repentance but corporate repentance for the whole Body of Christ. And that takes real hard, contending prayer, the kind of desperate prayer that breaks through the heavens and grabs hold of the Throne of God. That kind of prayer will bring us closer and closer to His holiness, and the closer we get, the more our sinful nature stands out in sharp contrast.

The Holy Ghost conviction that we need to birth a true outpouring is the kind that will break you. Knees will crack, hearts will break, and tears will flow. I'm not talking about poetic analogies – I'm talking about broken-hearted repentance that is so piercing that it will change your life forever.

Leonard Ravenhill once said that the only prayer God hears is desperate prayer. He must have gotten that from Elijah, a man who was just like us, but a man who knew what righteous, fervent effective prayer could do. Elijah was a rainmaker. If you want it to rain, you will have to pray like Elijah.

Anything short of that is just talk.

Drinking from the Bottle

Lately, I've been watching some video clips from one of my trips to Uganda. Watching them reminded me how great it felt to be in those services. That, and what a contrast they were to the services here back in the USA last Sunday. Boy, what a difference!

When I share these videos of wildly exuberant praise going on at these services, why is it that I don't get more of a rise from our quiet church brethren? There are some comments of approval but few cries of desperate hunger. They don't mind watching someone else dance around, but they don't want to do that themselves.

Over here, it is like sipping on a glass of wine, holding the glass between your index finger and thumb while your pinky hangs gracefully in the air. You get a bit of a nice warm feeling while you discuss the discreet variances of flavor and undertones of the wine. Nice. And quite cultured. Some people really like that kind of thing.

Over in Africa, however, it's like drinking the whole bottle in one long, upended pull. Same wine, but wow, what a rush!

I will always remember the Jesus Movement during the 70's when the Holy Ghost would fall on services every night so hard that you would literally be beside yourself, jumping up and down, hands raised to touch the heavens, shouting out praises to God at the top of your lungs. You couldn't help yourself. And that was the tame ones in the crowd! Maybe it's just me, but wouldn't you want to be immersed in a deluge of the Holy Spirit rather than sipping at the edge of the glass?

I see the same thing in Africa that I saw in the U.S. in 1970. And I see the same reaction from the churches. Back then, they patronized us long-haired Jesus Freaks as just a passing fad – a little crazy from drugs, but otherwise harmless. Now, that same Holy Ghost excitement that is happening in Africa is being explained away as emotionalism or as something that is happening "over there." *("After all, white men can't dance!")* Well then, explain the powerful outpouring of the Jesus Movement that we had over here. I'm white, and I was dancing.

Which do you want – the glass or the bottle? You want a nice warm buzz, or do you want to get sloppy drunk out of your mind? Are you so damned sophisticated that you can't tell the difference? Or are you so comfortable where you are that you don't want to shake things up. Or worse, turn them upside down.

We had it once. Why not again? Of course, that begs the question, how bad do we want it?

> "And they were all amazed, and were in doubt, saying one to another, What meaneth this? Others mocking said, These men are full of new wine." Acts 2:12,13
>
> "Awake, ye drunkards, and weep; and howl, all ye drinkers of wine, because of the new wine; for it is cut off from your mouth." Joel 1:5

Coming to Jordan

> " ... and a great multitude from Galilee followed him, and from Judaea, and from Jerusalem, and from Idumaea, and from beyond Jordan; and they about Tyre and Sidon, a great multitude, when they had heard what great things he did, came unto him." Mark 3:7,8

I went to a local church on Sunday that has about 3,000 members to see what it was like. Obviously, there must be something there that attracts so many people, and I wanted to see what it was. Someone told me that the pastor was a very good preacher, but there was a pause that hinted at something he wasn't telling me. Well, there are always issues no matter where you go, so I decided to see for myself.

While I would admit that the pastor was an impassioned speaker, I cannot say that he delivered an anointed message. Maybe it was an "off" day. But after several weeks of going to his church, I was left with little more than a series of interesting messages but no demonstration of the Spirit and power that Paul writes about in 1 Corinthians chapter 2. Nice, interesting, some great points ... but not anointed.

Do we not understand the difference anymore? Has it been so long since we have had the anointing of the Holy Spirit take control of our pulpits that we no longer recognize what we are missing? Yes, this pastor was very passionate, but that does not constitute the anointing of the Holy Ghost. Yes, it was very interesting, but that does not transform a human soul. Yes, I am sure he meant well, but that and 50 cents won't buy you a cup of coffee. Whatever happened to the outpouring of the power of God during services when the whole congregation was so immersed in the Spirit that they were not only transformed by the message but overwhelmed with the presence of God? Has it been so long that we have forgotten what that was like?

The thundering echoes of our men of God from the past have been reduced to the distant murmurs of a faded memory. Where are the great men and women of God that we once had? Where is the manifestation of the miracles of the Holy Spirit, the transforming power of anointed preaching of the Word of God, and the downpour of Holy Ghost conviction that sent a flood of repentant sinners to the altar? Where did God go? Has He left our churches to find fertile ground elsewhere?

I was told by a woman who attends this church that she loves her pastor because "he doesn't have a single judgmental bone in his body." Maybe that's what the problem is -- we have become "nice." Certainly, you can attract 3,000 people if you tell them what they want to hear, but are we so in tune with being "nice" that we have forsaken the commission God has given us to stand for the Truth? Have we become so focused on being "People That Love" that we no longer fear God? Make no mistake, when you leave the fear of God, you abandon not only the depths of wisdom and understanding but the strength and authority in God that goes with them. In our efforts to please people, we have lost our place in God. And with it, our anointing.

What caused so many people in Judea to drop everything they were doing and walk all the way to hear Jesus? It was because he spoke with authority under the anointing of the Holy Spirit. That is what feeds a hungry soul, not theologically correct sermons and complacent messages that are designed to entertain rather than convict. It takes Living Waters to quench a thirsty soul.

We are missing this today. I understand that many pastors and evangelists are trying their hardest to convey the Gospel as best they can.

But that is the problem, not the solution.

Answering a Fool

On two separate occasions, I have been approached by a couple of old acquaintances who have wanted to enlighten me with some deeper understandings. These two men are polar opposites in their beliefs, but both had the same intent. Like Job's comforters, they were just trying to help.

One is what I call an armchair theologian. You know the type. They never actually do anything; they just sit there and pontificate from their lofty position of deeper spiritual insights. After wading through page after page of his loquacious emails, I was left still wondering what his point was. Jesus was simple, but this guy makes it so complicated.

The other guy is a philosopher who feels he has gained spiritual insights into the "secret knowledge" of Gnosticism through the esoteric Johannine Gospel, which was supposedly secretly given to the Apostle John by Jesus, only to be revealed to the world when us lesser lights were ready to receive it. (Of course, only certain "enlightened" initiates have discovered this inside truth.) While this makes for fascinating stories of the Holy Grail and great fodder for books by Dan Brown, it is hardly worthy of consideration.

To the first, I would answer that the Bible says, "Knowledge puffeth up, but charity edifieth" (1 Cor. 8:1). I'm not interested in how much you know – go <u>do</u> something! The purpose of the Cross is not to learn a bunch of "stuff," but to have mercy on souls. Jesus died to save sinners, not hand out theological degrees.

To the other, I would ask why he is so relentlessly pursuing something he can never obtain. By its very definition, the whole philosophy of Gnosticism propagates the idea of an endless quest for deeper and deeper wisdom that is always just beyond the grasp of mortal man. Much like a carrot in front of a donkey. But when you find Jesus – the <u>real</u> Jesus – you find the fountain of Living Waters from which you will never thirst again. If you've found the Truth, then why would you have to keep searching for it?

As I searched the scriptures for how the Lord wanted me to answer these guys, I kept turning up dozens of scriptures that admonished me not to fall into the trap laid by either one of these purportedly well-meaning friends. While it is true that we are supposed to "contend for the faith," we are also told not to answer a fool in his folly nor reprove a scorner (Pro. 26:4, 23:9, 29:9). No matter what you say, they will not listen.

The essence of this issue goes back to the beginning of time. In the Garden of Eden, Man was given two choices: the Tree of the Knowledge of Good and Evil vs. the Tree of Life. Adam and Eve chose the wrong one. Sure, it was pleasant to look at (lust of the eyes), good for food (lust of the flesh), and a tree desired to make one wise (pride of life), but in its fruit were the seeds of death, for "to be carnally minded is death" (Rom. 8:6). But, hey, it sure made you feel good about yourself!

The Tree of Life, however, is not about you – how good you are, how smart you are, how "deep" you are, or how powerful you are. To eat off that tree means you must humble yourself before God and lend yourself to His wisdom, power, and righteousness. That pretty much shoots down any spiritual pride you might be hanging onto for yourself.

All heresy has the distinct purpose of minimizing sin and promoting the three lusts of the Tree of Knowledge. It is always in direct conflict with the crucified subjection to the will of God.

So why are they so vehement about pushing their agenda on others? The second Psalm starts with, "Why do the heathen rage and the people imagine a vain thing?." The Psalmist answers in verse 3 that it is to break the bands of Holy Ghost conviction off them and the cords of subjection to God's righteousness. That was what Satan tried to do also, and it has led to the downfall of untold masses of humanity.

After searching all his life, the wisest man in the world concluded that the whole duty of man was to fear God and keep His commandments (Eccl. 12:13).

As for wisdom? Job 28 gives the best answer:

"But where shall wisdom be found? And where is the place of understanding? ...
And unto man he said, Behold, the fear of the Lord, that is wisdom; and to depart from evil is understanding."

Job 28:12, 28

Jehoshaphat

> *"Now Jehoshaphat had riches and honor in abundance, and joined affinity with Ahab."* 2 Chronicles 18:1

Ol' Jehoshaphat was a pretty good king, but he was as dumb as a rock. Nice guy, but not very bright.

Judah had well over a million men of war, so it is no wonder that all the nations around gave them tribute. Nobody wanted to mess with Jehoshaphat. It is also not surprising that Ahab, the wicked king of Israel, sidled up to him to ask for help against the Syrians.

I can just hear Ahab now, "Hey cuz, ol' buddy! You know, you and I, we're family. How 'bout a little help here to retake Ramoth-Gilead."

No, you're not family! Israel had left the family of God when they decided to worship golden calves instead of the Lord God Jehovah. If you look at this spiritually, this is the worldly Church trying to integrate itself with the true Church of God. Yeah, you look the same, but Ahab was not of the lineage of David, and their religion was not of God.

So Jehoshaphat decides to be a nice guy and help his poor misguided "brethren" in the battle. Now, when Ahab called upon the 400 prophets of Baal to bless their endeavors, you'd think that maybe that should have given Jehoshaphat a clue. And when a true prophet of God had the courage to prophesy against it but was tossed into prison, that should have told Jehoshaphat that it was time to get out of there. Nope. Not Jehoshaphat. He went along with it and almost got killed as a result.

Not only that, but as a result of the terrible defeat, he no longer had the strength of his once-mighty army to resist the Ammonites, Moabites, and Edomites that were now emboldened to come against Judah. What happened to your million men, Jehoshaphat? You lost your power and strength when you decided to join forces with the worldly Church of Ahab, and now you have become a sitting duck for the devil to attack and destroy the Church.

And it doesn't end there. Because of his continued affinity with the world, not only did God break his works in Ezion-Geber, but the heritage of righteousness was corrupted. His lack of strength, resolve, and godly fear allowed wickedness to enter the next generation. Jehoram, his wicked son, married Ahab's daughter and murdered his brothers who were righteous, and that sealed the destruction of the next generations of the kings of Judah, ultimately leading to their captivity in Babylon.

The message should be as clear as transparent glass. But what do we see today? In our efforts to be "nice" so that we are embracive to others and to show love and not offend anyone, we have blurred the stark differences between the holy and the profane. We no longer fear God. Leonard Ravenhill once proclaimed that we have more of Hollywood than holiness in our churches. And he said that a generation ago! It has gotten worse since then.

If we, as the Body of Christ, follow the same path of Jehoshaphat, we will end up with the same results.

A Glimpse

There's a lot of stuff that I don't understand. I suppose I never will. It's comforting to know that someday it will all be made clear, but that day is a ways off.

I grew up alone on the streets. I wasn't good; I wasn't bad; I just was. The great meaning in Life had always eluded me – I wasn't even sure there was a meaning -- so I made the conscious decision to refuse to believe in God. But for some unknown reason, He was watching over me, and when He had enough of my rebellious ways, He ended it just like that. He made me know He was there.

It's been over 50 years since then -- a lifetime in anyone's book. After all this time, I still wonder why He did that for me. I wasn't anything special. I was not exceptionally talented in anything. Neither did I possess any true strength of character or any emotional depth. Just a kid wandering around wondering what Life was all about. But for some kind of grace, He saved me, and I am still saved.

I've met a lot of people who have genuine depths of character. Some of them have a magical quality to their souls. Some are so magnanimous in their love for people that I feel like a toad in comparison. Some have been gifted with the ability to see past the veneer of this life, whether in love, art, or some other form of expression, and use their talents to transform to reach out to touch the hearts of those around them.

I don't have that. I'm stuck in my own flat universe, doing the best I can to do the work that is set before me. I guess God looked at me and figured that while maybe I wasn't anything special, at least I'd keep at the task. Sometimes I feel like a sheepdog – I don't know what it is that I'm doing or why, and I don't care about the reward -- I just want to keep working.

Why, then, do people who seem to have so much wonderful value as human beings not grasp the one thing that will determine their everlasting destiny? Why does God shower them with such riches for such a short time only to spend the rest of Eternity in torment? And then some people, who possess so few redeeming qualities in this life, get to spend forever in Heaven?

When I was very young in the Lord, I asked Him why do some people get saved and some people don't? He answered me directly – it was the very first time that I heard God actually speak to me -- "Some people care, and some people don't," He said, "It's as simple as that." To this day, that is the most profound thing I have ever heard.

I should leave it at that, but I just can't. Why Lord? Why do so many people who possess such grace in this life not care about the one thing that really matters? And why is it that I care? I certainly did not choose this – You chose it for me. Why me?

I don't suppose I'll ever know – at least not on this side of Eternity. But this much I do know. God is real. He is the master of all mysteries. He knows all, and He knows why, but He keeps His own counsel.

To us, He gives a glimpse at that which we cannot understand or explain, but He does give us that glimpse.

Yawn

Some time ago, I called around to a bunch of the local churches to see if I could come and share some of the exciting things that have been happening in Africa. I told them upfront that I was not looking for money but just for an opportunity to spread the fire that was starting to burn over there. I even offered to send some of the journals I had written during the trips there so that they could see what I was talking about, smell the smoke, and feel the heat. Seemed like a reasonable request to me – read my stuff and see if you would like me to come to tell the story.

Initially, I had put the journals together as a series of small booklets, so I could present them to businesses looking for a tax write-off somewhere, but that went over like a lead balloon. The Lord once spoke to me when I tried to get support from the churches, "They will not support you. You get your support from Me." Okay. But does that include businesses too? Remember the verse, "Go to the ant thou sluggard"? Aren't I supposed to do something at least?

Well, apparently not. Just sit and wait on Him. Seems counterintuitive, but that's the message I'm getting. If He wants me to go somewhere, He'll send the money. And if He doesn't send the money? Well, then maybe He doesn't want me to go. Simple. Takes all the sweat out of it.

Okay, so not being content to just sit there, I changed my course to instead asking the churches around here if I could just come and share about the incredible outpouring of the Spirit of God in Africa, how tens of thousands have been saved, hundreds healed, and how the power of God is transforming and igniting the churches over there. I figured everybody would want to hear about that, especially if I offered to send the booklets first so they could check it out. No money! Free of charge! I'll sing for my supper. If you don't like the message, then give me a bologna sandwich, a pat on the back, and send me on my way.

Stupid me. Yes, there have been a few who were happy for me to send the booklets (nobody's called back yet, but give 'em time), but I also began to run into churches that would rudely brush me off with comments like, "We're not interested in that. <click>" Huh? Am I missing something here? You're not interested in that?

One place responded with a polite inquiry into whether I belonged to their particular denomination. Excuse me? The power of Almighty God is crashing down over there, and you want to check the Holy Spirit's credentials? I can see where you might look askance at me – yeah, I'm a little rough around the edges – but don't you even want to check and see if this is really God? Aren't you afraid of missing out on the greatest move of God of all time?

"Nope. Have a nice day. <click>" (Actually, they didn't even wish me a nice day.)

And people wonder why God would send revival to Africa first and not to America? It sounds to me like we fit the description of the Church of Laodicea all too well. We're just not hungry enough.

And that's a little scary.

The Esther Church

> *"Then Mordecai commanded to answer Esther, Think not with thyself that thou shalt escape in the king's house, more than all the Jews.*
>
> *For if thou altogether holdest thy peace at this time, then shall there enlargement and deliverance arise to the Jews from another place; but thou and thy father's house shall be destroyed: and who knoweth whether thou art come to the kingdom for such a time as this?"*
> *Esther 4:14, 15*

In the Book of Esther, we see two pictures of the Church – the Esther church, residing in the palace under the obvious blessings of God, and the Mordecai church, which sits under oppression and persecution.

Esther was perfect in her natural beauty. Her refusal of worldly enhancements endeared her to the King, who loved her above all others and made her his queen. She is the very embodiment of the Bride of Christ, beautiful in grace, entering into the blessings of God honestly and humbly. Proverbs 22:11 says that he that loves pureness of heart, the king shall be his friend. Esther was a perfect picture of that pureness of heart.

Mordecai, however, sat on the other side of the palace walls. As a devout Jew, he would bow to no one other than God Almighty, so when wicked Haman rode by, whose ambitions knew no bounds, he considered Mordecai's refusal to bow the ultimate insult. Haman, like Satan, aspired to be like the Most High, and was determined to gain that power using the demonic methods of deceit and murder. When he saw Mordecai the Jew refusing to give him homage, his hatred for the people of God welled up to overflowing. He ordered Mordecai hanged on the gallows and conspired to destroy the entire race of Jews.

So, Mordecai went to the only place of refuge he knew was sure – he sat in dust and ashes at the king's gate.

It is not enough to say that we know God and trust that God will always deliver us. That is mere presumption. Presumption does not seem that bad when times are good. If it works, great; if it doesn't, oh well, no great loss. But when utter destruction and severe persecution are looming over you, you have no room for chance, and all those great and swelling words of love, peace, and overflowing blessings wear a little thin.

Mordecai knew that he needed an answer from the Throne of God, and he was willing to sit at His gate in fasting and prayer until God moved. Even when honored by the king to be led through the town by Haman, proclaiming the honor bestowed upon Mordecai by the king, he went right back to his sackcloth and ashes. So often, we as Christians will seek the face of God for an answer in times of trouble, but as soon as we feel the winds of victory begin to blow across our face, we quit and assume that God will take it the rest of the way. Not so with Mordecai. He was determined to pray it all the way through to victory.

As a young Christian, I was taught to pray like a warrior and stand before God in holy boldness and determination, claiming my answer before God. "One of us is going to move," I would cry out to God, "and it's not going to be me!" When you pray like that, be prepared to be tested, but like Mordecai, you will not quit until you get your answer. The definition of Faith is not believing that God <u>can</u> do something – any fool can believe that. It's believing that He <u>will</u> do it because you will not let go until He does!

While the people of God outside the palace had been determined for destruction, Esther was at ease in the palace and oblivious to their plight. Only the sight of Mordecai in sackcloth got her to realize something was wrong. The challenge he answered her with was severe – march into the King's Throne Room and plead for the deliverance of her persecuted brethren. It was an act of ultimate courage, for if the King did not accept you, your only fate was death.

The Throne Room was not a place to wander in mindlessly. If so on earth with earthly kings, how much more with God Almighty? And yet, because we stand in the grace of God, we know without a doubt that God will hold out the golden scepter, but it takes a certain holy boldness to march all the way up to the Throne (we are not talking regular prayer here), and only righteousness in the fear of God will give you that kind of holy boldness and victory.

Esther could have made excuses to get around Mordecai's request. She could have ignored the problems her brethren would face outside the walls and gone about with her life of peace and blessings. But she didn't. She took upon herself the challenge that has always been placed upon those in the "Esther" church to defend her persecuted brethren and, taking her life in her hands, go to the Throne of God for their deliverance.

But do we in America, as the most blessed and prosperous church that has ever been, hear the call of Mordecai? Do we do anything more than peer over the castle walls and muse amongst ourselves at how terrible it must be for those in third-world countries who not only live in a state of poverty that we cannot imagine but defend the Gospel with their very lives?

Sadly, the answer is no. Oh yes, we support our missionaries who have to take months off from ministry to come and plead with us for enough finances to subsist. We write a check and hope that all will be well, and we have a picture in our minds of a nice little missionary hut somewhere "over there." But do we really know and understand the intensity of the hardships they are facing? Are we really willing to take upon ourselves the same role that Esther did?

Mordecai's answer to her is chilling. He knew God was going to deliver the Jews somehow because he knew he was not going to let go of the horns of the altar until God did. But if Esther did not come to their aid at such a time, she would face destruction. God had placed her in this position for just such a time as this. She was part of the plan of salvation for God's people. Is America any different?

It is amazing what we can accomplish when we yield to what God has called us to do, whether inside the palace or outside the walls. It was not the threat of destruction but rather the brotherly love that marks us as true Christians that Esther responded to. "If I perish, I perish," she replied as she prepared to present herself before the king and went in to touch the golden scepter. Touching the golden scepter is that point of prayer we come to when, having done all we can, we submit to the mercy of God and experience that breakthrough in the prayer room. Only true prayer warriors know what that is like. And that is the point when your deliverance begins.

God has a plan, and He calls us to answer the call. We can busy ourselves with our own lives and never notice what happens elsewhere, feigning ignorance and the importance of those things surrounding us, but the call comes to us from over the walls.

An old man sits down there, slumped over in his cry to God, covered in garments of affliction, soiled by the dust of humility before God, and rocking back in forth in the agony of prayer. When we look closer, we see that it is our cousin, the persecuted church, afflicted by the forces of darkness and slated for destruction. We sigh and feel bad for him, but will we take upon ourselves the call to battle?

Esther made her choice without hesitation.

Fat and Lazy

> "... I am rich, and increased with goods, and have need of nothing ..." (Rev 3:17)

I was at a High School baseball game not long ago, and as I looked around at the crowd, I noticed how many people were fat. Not just "beefy" or "heavy," but plain ol' fat!

This is not an isolated scene but is endemic across America. How'd we get so fat? I don't remember it being like this when I was growing up or even as recently as 20 years ago. Maybe I just wasn't paying attention, but regardless, Americans have lost that image of being lean, mean, tough, and hard-working. At some point, we were paying attention to something else that captured our attention, and we got soft and fat.

Our physical condition is a perfect reflection of our spiritual condition. Our pastors preached a different message a generation or so ago, and our congregations were much more vibrant with a solid spirit. But now, our preachers have turned into nice guys, and our churches have turned to mush. We've become soft and fat and lazy.

I'm sure many church-oriented people will object to that, just as those who have given up looking for a good church will probably agree with it.

I have spent a lot of time in Africa, where the people are desperately hungry to see the power of God working in their church. So much so that they will walk for 10 to 12 hours, sleep on the floor of the church, and be content with rice and beans just so they can hear the Word of God preached under the anointing of the Holy Ghost. Americans are not that hungry, nor are they willing to pay that kind of price for anything.

As a result, in Africa, souls are getting saved, supernaturally healed, and ignited with the Fire of God. Churches there are being transformed from sleepy little country churches to on-fire Spirit-ignited soul winners. Revival is beginning to break out in Africa, but not in America.

I've noticed that almost everyone in Africa is skinny. Hmmm.

We used to be just like them once upon a time. What happened? Did we get so comfortable that we no longer needed God? Did our blessings kill us?

Did our fat plug our ears up so that we can no longer hear the reproof of the Word of God, and so, instead of snapping out of it, we justify our religious institutions, our spiritual slackness, and our decided lack of the fear of God. We have plenty of alternate theologies to explain away our spiritual laziness and justify our apostasy. Our leaders are all graduates of theologically-correct institutions and are armed with libraries of scholastic credentials, so they must be right ... aren't they?

But we can no longer hear the searing reproof of the Word of God. We have become scorners who are deaf and can no longer repent.

"And he said, Go, and tell this people, Hear ye indeed, but understand not; and see ye indeed, but perceive not. Make the heart of this people fat, and make their ears heavy, and shut their eyes; lest they see with their eyes, and hear with their ears, and understand with their heart, and convert, and be healed." (Isaiah 6:9,10)

Turned Unto Fables

"A religion of mere emotion and sensationalism is the most terrible of all curses that can come upon any people. The absence of reality is sad enough, but the aggravation of pretense is a deadly sin." -
Samuel Chadwick

Sound like any of the churches you've been to lately? Or like some of the televangelists that swarm the airwaves with their sensationalism? Or like our new wave of "revivalists" who lead us like Pied Pipers to emotional displays of excitement rather than bringing us to the altar of repentance, the only place where true revival can be found?

Somewhere in our pursuit of religious goals, bigger churches, and more prosperous ministries, we compared price tags and chose the one that promised the biggest bang for the cheapest price. It was a simple decision. Why labor and agonize for long lonely nights in secret with God for intangible results claimed by an invisible faith when for the cheap price of instant sensationalism, we can have the proven attraction of a Hollywood extravaganza?

- We have traded the agony of deep travail in prayer for a cheap and easy "name it and claim it." We "speak the word" like sorcerers expecting God to jump at the snap of our fingers to bring us blessings, but our hearts are strangely silent for the things that God cries for.
- All-night prayer meetings these days mean a half hour for each of us shared for a few hours or so, not the desperate cries for lost souls that rang out until the dawn broke.
- Contending before God and storming the Throne of Grace in spiritual warfare is now a lost art (at which we breathe a sigh of relief for its loss). Our revival prayer meetings today are merely a subdued time of murmured prayers and shared insights with a backdrop of praise music instead of the times of intense warfare that used to crash the gates of Heaven for revival in times past.

- We have left the secret place of the Most High for a more "professional" production with lights, glitter, and smoke.
- The altars of repentance that once beckoned to lost souls desperate for Salvation have now become magnets for "pity" lines to assuage our weakened church members that they are "loved."
- Our focus has turned away from the desperate masses of the lost and has been redirected to a self-oriented doctrine of prosperity, blessings, and wealth ... for ourselves.
- We have broken the constrictions of strong old-fashioned doctrine for the warm and friendly openness of ecumenism, not only with the harlot church but even with Hindus and Muslims.
- We have turned Hell from an everlasting furnace of torment that awaits the multitudes into a place of discomfort that only a very few will ever go to.
- We have dismissed the fearlessness of holy boldness as rude and unbecoming because it is too unsettling to our comfortable ways. Instead, we have trained our pastors to be nice, warm, and accommodating so they won't offend anyone.
- We are more concerned with being conciliatory than being a lightning rod of God's judgments, and so we swarm to those who claim to have a "prophetic spirit" and will tell us what we want to hear, but we are repulsed by brash prophets who carry forth a word of rebuke.
- The Love of God is no longer the keeping of God's commandments but is pictured as a warm, fuzzy emotion that, along with a cheap Grace, is leading the Church into a lukewarm apostasy.
- The Fear of God is no longer the fear, trembling, and dread of the Almighty but has become "awesome respect."

In short, we have become sophisticated. And this is what is found in the Assemblies of God, the Pentecostals, the Baptists, and the new rash of evangelical and charismatic churches – the ones who are supposed to be alive!

Does anyone realize how desperate we are for a revival? Not a churchy imitation of fake sensationalism like we see in today's "revivalists," but a God-fearing, Heaven-sent, flesh-crucifying broken cry for the holiness of God? But who among us are desperate enough to drop to their knees and pour their hearts out at the altar of repentance for God to have mercy on us? Who among us will contend before God in secret travail until God answers? Has our desperate passion for the lost died?

Are there any of us who realize how far we have drifted? We depend upon a carnal production rather than the unction of the Spirit. Our preachers cover up the loss with manufactured speeches that are passed off for sermons that are forgotten five minutes after the congregation has passed through the doors. They depend more upon their scholastic abilities than a crucified dependence on the anointing of the Holy Ghost. As a result, they have lost the power that once thundered over their pulpits. Were any lives changed, any hearts broken, any sin exposed and cleansed, any souls saved? Did the Blood flow?

Does anyone care?

"And I sought for a man among them, that should make up the hedge, and stand in the gap before me for the land, that I should not destroy it: but I found none." (Ezekiel 22:30)

"For the time will come when they will not endure sound doctrine; but after their own lusts shall they heap to themselves teachers, having itching ears; And they shall turn away their ears from the truth, and shall be turned unto fables." (2 Timothy 4:3,4)

It is not a question of whether we agree or not, whether we will utter our "Amens" or bob our heads up and down – it is a matter of what you will do about it.

Talk, Talk, Talk

I have been going through a period of still waters. During that time, I've listened to the many streams of Christian dialogue that run in every direction. Some focus on the threat of Islam and Sharia Law to our American way of life, others warn of impending cataclysmic judgments, and others warn of promises of revival and coming blessings to the Church. Many talk about how dead the churches are (the <u>other</u> churches, that is). And, of course, there are innumerable conspiracy issues that must be exposed to the world.

We postulate and pontificate, we predict and prophesy, and we rant and rave while we argue and debate. Some of us sound like rabble-rousers whose primary mission in life is to illuminate the unenlightened, while others sound like naïve throwbacks to the hippie generation with their prophetic words of peace, love, and blessings. We're all supposed to believe the same thing, but it sure looks like we are viewing it from very different-looking glasses.

After a while, it all begins to sound like just so much noise.

Maybe I'm not seeing this any better than anyone else, but it sure seems that the distilled end of all of this only ends up with the same thing: lots of talk, plenty of noise, clouds of dust in the air, but little substance. We are a generation that talks itself to death. Email, Facebook, Twitter, Blogs, SMS, cell phones, (did I miss anything?) Our kids are addicted to texting, and we old folks are catching the disease.

We forward conspiracy emails that we have never bothered to verify to all our Outlook contacts and Facebook Friends and then spend our time berating anyone who objects. Some of us rise to a frenzy over a purported crisis that some celebrity sensationalist has convinced us is coming upon us and raises the cry that civilization as we know it is about to collapse.

Others call upon their "prophetic spirit" to speak into the wind with promises of "peace and safety" and ethereal claims that God will send us revival. Oh, and by the way, God is going to prosper you and use you in some great supernatural way. Just so you know.

But do we ever DO anything?

Where are we going with all this? What is it that each of us wants to see done? Is there a point? Or are we running around in circles proclaiming our own particular "inside knowledge" while the issues that God is really concerned about are passing by? The Bible says that without a vision, my people perish (Proverbs 29:18). What is the goal that we are working toward? Or is it just to hear ourselves talk? Are we just clouds without rain and wells without water? Sometimes I wonder.

An empty drum makes the most noise, as the saying goes. Even the Bible says that talk is cheap (Prov. 14:23). Sorry, but after a while, all that noise -- the proclaimings and prophesyings, the rantings and warnings, and theological pontificating -- begins to sound like an empty wind rustling through the leaves of the Tree of the Knowledge of Good and Evil. It sounds good, looks good, tastes good, and it is desired to make one wise. But does it DO anything?

Now you may say, "But these things are really true!" Well, maybe they are, and maybe they aren't, but until we get past words alone, they remain, as Paul puts it in 1st Corinthians 13, nothing more than a sounding brass and a tinkling cymbal (1 Cor. 13:1). I'm not saying that we shouldn't make a noise and shout about issues that are important to us, but there comes a point where we have to be converted into action, or we are left with nothing but noise. It is not the hearers that are just before God, but the doers. (Romans 2:13)

We are saved by faith, but faith without works is dead (James 2:20). Left to itself, it is nothing more than presumption. Hope is the anchor of our soul (Heb. 6:19), but hope by itself is nothing more than wishful thinking. Neither Faith nor Hope is important as Charity.

Charity is the very essence of the Cross. It is the purpose to which we have been called. It is the one thing Jesus asked us to do before He left us. His last request had nothing to do with building your ministry, your spiritual position, your church, your theological wisdom, or how much stuff you know. He asked us to do one thing, and we have gone about doing everything else but that thing.

His last words to us in Mark 16:15 were, *"Go ye into all the world, and preach the gospel to every creature."*

Simple. Go win souls.

*"...I know thy works, and thy labor, and thy patience, ...
nevertheless I have somewhat against thee, because thou hast left thy
first love.*

*Remember therefore from whence thou art fallen, and repent, and do
the first works; or else I will come unto thee quickly, and will remove
thy candlestick out of his place, except thou repent.
(Revelations 2:4,5)*

Sandbar

I've been spending a few days alone down at the river, just hanging around. This morning, I was walking downstream and crossed over onto one of the sandbars that are so frequent in this shallow, flat-bottom river. Short-lived weeds pop up all over these sandbars for a fleeting gasp of air and sunshine before the river rises and the next surge of water rushes down to wash them all away again. Before they are swept away, they rush to sprout seed pods for the next generation in a continuing struggle to survive.

It made me think about Nature's desperate cling to life. Even in the harshest conditions, there is that ever-present push to sustain life and press through regeneration. It's like a universal war between the animate and the inanimate. There is a force of Nature at work here that is not natural, but that comes from beyond the visible. Something is pushing that drive for life that we see all around us. That something has to be God. What else could it be?

I walked a little farther down the sandbar, my feet crunching the gravelly sand. It was obvious that it was not too long ago that the water had rushed over this spot and washed everything away. There were a few tracks from deer, raccoons, and three-toed cranes but little else. Even the weeds looked as if they had almost been pulled out from their tenuous grasp in the sand. But as I looked closer, I noticed some small colorful flowers in the bushes. And then some more. And some more. Here in the midst of a harsh strand of rocks and sand with little nourishment and a short hope for the future, were these little bursts of beauty and color. It was as if to say that not only has God provided the miracle of Life in a cold, barren universe but has punctuated it with the evidence of His love for us with this unheralded witness.

Everyone faces challenges in getting through life. Sometimes we wonder where we are going and why. And where is God in all of this? I can't say I know the where and why of everything. Sometimes life can get tough, and there doesn't always seem to be any answers. But standing on the barren sand of this sandbar that is poised for the next purging flood that will wash everything away, I am reassured by the evidence around me, as if God was peeking at me through those little bursts of tiny flowers, that He is there, and all is well.

Ten Pieces of Silver

> *"Either what woman having ten pieces of silver, if she lose one piece, doth not light a candle, and sweep the house, and seek diligently till she find it? And when she hath found it, she calleth her friends and her neighbors together, saying, Rejoice with me; for I have found the piece which I had lost. Likewise, I say unto you, there is joy in the presence of the angels of God over one sinner that repenteth."*
>
> *(Luke 15:8-10)*

As I get older, I find myself going through the same thing this woman went through. Where is that thing that I just laid down a moment ago? Where are my glasses? What happened to that pen I just had in my hand? It was here just a moment ago. Am I getting stupid as the days progress, or am I just getting old?

Or am I just like the Church?

We can take comfort that we still have nine pieces of silver and that the tenth piece is around here somewhere. It'll turn up sooner or later. In the meantime, we have many other things to do that are more important right now.

Or are they?

Many of us may lament the loss of one piece of silver and will light a candle to find it, but if it doesn't show up, we are satisfied that at least we made an effort to find it. We have tall white steeples to let everyone know where our churches are, we put our church in the local Church Directory for everyone to find us, and we've even put a sign out front to invite them in. We have lit our candles and are satisfied that we have done our best. But few of us are willing to sweep the house and turn it upside down in a desperate search for that one lost piece of silver, that one lost sheep.

The Lord doesn't think like us. To Him, that missing piece of silver is every bit as important as the other nine. He would rather leave the 99 sheep to go find that one missing lamb than console Himself with the loss of even one.

It's a matter of focus. What is the passion of your life? What are you really focused on? A true burden for souls gazes at neither self nor church but looks past all that to focus on only one thing – lost souls.

The Church, however, is becoming increasingly fixated on herself and, as a result, has lost that burden for that one lost piece of silver. She will light a candle but will not sweep the house and search diligently until she finds it.

She is too busy with other things.

> *"Then shall ye begin to say, We have eaten and drunk in thy presence, and thou hast taught in our streets. But he shall say, I tell you, I know you not whence ye are; depart from me, all ye workers of iniquity." (Luke 13:26, 27)*

Learning How to Die

"God is not trying to change you. He's trying to kill you!"

I read this today, and it rang a bell in me. It isn't changing that I need to worry about. I've worked my whole Christian life trying to change myself into the man of God I have pictured as my goal in life. No, I have to die.

This is not about being a better Christian or volunteering more at church. It's not even about reading more Bible or fasting and praying more so that you will become a stronger man of God. It is not about you. It's about others. It's about giving up your vision of yourself and surrendering to Him.

Many folks look at me and think I've got this whole thing all wrapped up in a neat package, but I'm as scared as the next guy about letting go and stepping into the unknown. How do you drop all the stabilizing things in your life and step off the edge of the cliff? Is that what it means to die? Do I just have to shut off the switch that is labeled "Me"?

No one realizes how scared every time I am called to stand up before even the smallest groups of people in the remotest of villages. Every time. No matter how many thousands of messages I have preached, how many churches that have been ignited, or hundreds of people that have been saved and healed, I still find myself crying, "Lord, will I be able to deliver your Word this time with the Anointing that will change their lives? When they ask me to pray for them, will they actually get healed? Will You show up? 'Cause, honestly, Lord, I don't know how to do this."

No, this is about dying, not growing.

When I look at myself, I can see with sharp clarity all the warts and pimples I have. I struggle with all kinds of stuff that I'd rather not tell anyone about. I don't have enough faith. I don't pray hard enough. I hate fasting. I catch myself thinking about the wrong stuff, saying the wrong things, and leaning in the wrong directions. Lord, I don't know if you've been paying attention, but I'm not the guy you think I am. I can point to the guys who really are better than me, who could do a much better job than me. I honestly have no idea what I'm doing.

But those prayers are all answered the same way. I hear that pregnant silence, His breathing punctuated with the sound of Him patiently drumming His fingers, waiting for me while I'm looking around, asking if He can find somebody else.

So I swallow (gulp), take a deep breath, and say, I know I am not worthy - and will <u>never</u> be worthy. I don't know how to be some righteous Holy Joe, some great supernatural powerhouse in God, or how to lead your people. I don't know how to organize a deeply theological sermon, don't know how to do miracles, don't know how to deal with people's emotions, how to preach, how to pastor, or even be a great Christian. I don't know anything.

But here am I, Lord.

Send me.

Tied to the Dock

My Dad used to tell me, "Son, you never know what you can do until you try." I have found that to be so true.

I guess the lesson for me to consider is to ask myself, what is the worst thing that can happen? And then go ahead and jump off the edge of the cliff and trust God to catch me. Or, I could just stand there looking down into the chasm and never take a chance to do anything. If I have to choose, I will pick the first one. If you don't take a step of faith, you will never go anywhere.

I realize that not everyone is as adventurous (or crazy) as I am. Some folks do not put such a high value on breaking the routines of a mundane life -- and I concede that they very well may be right – but in the face of Eternity, I feel like I want to do something, anything, and I want to do it while I can. Ecclesiastes 11:2 tells us to give while we can because we never know what is coming. That speaks to me about sacrifice now, not later. Do something now before the opportunity passes.

Several years ago, the Lord gave me a vision for a certain pastor who was stuck in his ties to his denomination. He was afraid to let go and step outside their constraints even when the Lord was leading in a very different direction. Now, I may not be much for following rules, but I do realize that, for many people, rules offer structure and strength. Nevertheless, there comes a point where that structure can constrict the free flow of the Spirit of God.

The vision God gave me for him was of an old-fashioned sailing ship tied up to a rickety old wharf. The ship looked like it was in great shape, but the wharf was little more than a patched-up bunch of old rotten boards jutting out into the water. It looked like it would fall apart at any moment. He was that ship, and his denomination was that wharf.

The ship was tethered to the wharf by some thick hawsers – big, fat ropes. I got the feeling that the thick ropes that tied him to his denomination gave this pastor a feeling of security.

The ship was safe in the harbor and tied securely to the dock. What could go wrong? But the message to that pastor was that if he did not cut the ropes and spread his sails, he would never go anywhere in the Lord.

Sure, it can be dangerous past the mouth of the harbor. Pirates, storms, hurricanes, whirlpools, and all sorts of dangers are waiting out there. But there are also great adventures in the Lord and places you've never been to that are just waiting for you to trust the Lord, cut the ropes, and let the Holy Spirit fill your sails.

You never know what you can do until you try. That's true, Dad. But many never try.

When we all stand before the Judgment Bar of God to give account for our lives, will it be said of you that, like Peter, at least you got out of the boat and got your feet wet? Or were you content to sit on the sidelines and watch others carry the ball? And let me say that it is not the guy doing the preaching that is doing the work and fighting the battle – it's the ones on their knees in their Prayer Closet. There is no victory in the pulpit until the battle has been fought and won in the prayer room … and we are all called to pray.

I have seen many friends get sick and die in the last several years. In many of those cases, they had slacked off in serving the Lord, content to cruise along at church. Many would not go to church because they felt it was dead, but neither did they offer anything as an alternative. And then, all of a sudden, they were dying. Certainly, as many have told me, it was a wake-up call for them, but too late for them to do anything about it.

Thank God for His enduring mercy in snapping them out of their slumber, but Lord, let me do something for you now while I can. I want no regrets, no do-overs, no "wish-I-would-have's." I may not be able to do what we perceive as great and mighty works in God, but allow me, like the woman in Mark 14 who washed your feet, to do what I can while I can.

But be ye doers of the word, and not hearers only, deceiving your own selves. (James 1:22)

Things I Don't Understand

There are things I have trouble understanding about God. And there are some things that I wish were not true. There's not much I can do about it, but that's the way it is.

I don't understand how holy God is. It says in Job that the heavens are not clean in His sight (Job 15:15). How can that be? Yeah, I can understand that our atmosphere is full of dust, ozone, fluorocarbons, and other ugly stuff that we spit out, but in the vast virginal expanse of space, isn't that all pristine? There's nothing there! And yet even the that is not clean to Him.

And then He says, "... how much more abominable is Man who drinks iniquity like water?" So we need a Savior. I get that part; I just don't think the mind of man is capable of grasping the holiness of God. Which is okay until you get to the part about Hell.

Faith has never been easy for me. Even after 52 years of walking with God, I am still amazed that He is really, really there. The idea of Eternity has always been beyond my grasp because it just doesn't make sense to my carnal mind. Like most little kids, I grew up with a basic belief in God – I didn't know much about Him but just naturally accepted the idea that He was up there somewhere. Some old guy with a long beard up there watching us. But when I reached 12 years old, I began to wonder where He was and why He was hiding from us. I went through an intense struggle until, out of frustration, I decided that the idea of God just didn't make sense. We've all been kidding ourselves. The problem was, however, that if God wasn't there, neither was life after death. Maybe eternity was there, but it was bound to be a cold, lifeless expanse of nothingness forever. I had a problem with that. There had to be something more to life than what met the eye, but my rational mind couldn't accept it. Was it wishful thinking? Fairy tales for old ladies and little kids? Fabricated answers for the unanswerable questions?

And then God revealed Himself to me. Three times. (I had a hard time believing it the first two times). But it was real. I didn't know who God was, which one He was, or how to find him, but I knew He was there. And then I got saved. I had never heard about being "saved" or "born again," but I knew something deep and dramatic had happened to me, and I was changed forever.

I have had over 50 years of supernatural experiences with God, and yet He is still a mystery to me. That's okay; it's enough to know that it is all real -- I'll figure it all out when I get to the other side — but there are still some things that I don't like and don't understand. Like the reality of Hell. And why most people will choose to ignore it.

If I could write the book on Eternity, I'd like to put in a clause that everybody gets a second chance once they face Judgment and finally realize it was all true. Or maybe just burn them for a couple of hundred years or so before snuffing them out. Something – anything – that will get around the horror of an eternal place of torment. But I didn't get to write the story.

So what can I do? That's what really bugs me. Sometimes I feel so powerless. I want to rip open the curtains of reality and shout to the whole world that there is a final and eternal judgment that everyone will face, and if they don't choose Salvation, they will be lost forever. I have read that, counting the 8 billion people alive today, there have been 15 billion people who have ever lived. About half of all the people who have ever lived are here today. And most of them have no idea what is waiting for them. Except for the Christians. But most of them live like they have no idea either.

Yeah, I don't like the idea of Hell, but there it is in all its flaming glory, written into the Word of God for all of us to read. I don't know what to do or how to do it. And that's what really bothers me.

We have had some great men of God in the past who were endued with incredible power in God, but they are all gone. Today we have a lot of nice guys in the pulpits, but we're missing the thundering echoes of the power and authority in God to expose to an unbelieving world that God is not only real, but He can save.

We need a revival today more than we have ever needed one.

"Oh that thou wouldest rend the heavens, that thou wouldest come down, that the mountains might flow down at thy presence, as when the melting fire burneth, the fire causeth the waters to boil, to make thy name known to thine adversaries, that the nations may tremble at thy presence!" (Isaiah 64:1,2)

Amen.

A Pot of Oil

> *"Now there cried a certain woman of the wives of the sons of the prophets unto Elisha, saying, Thy servant my husband is dead; and thou knowest that thy servant did fear the LORD: and the creditor is come to take unto him my two sons to be bondmen.*
>
> *And Elisha said unto her, what shall I do for thee? Tell me, what hast thou in the house? And she said, Thine handmaid hath not anything in the house, save a pot of oil."* (2Ki 4:1,2)

Here is a picture of the church in a time of spiritual recession. Her husband had been a prophet, so she had at one time known the ways of the Lord, but now he was gone, and she sat alone in poverty, powerless to save her sons from bondage. Elisha did not give her money but instead asked her what she still possessed in herself.

A pot of oil. Just a residue of the anointing that she once had in abundance. How like the Widow of Zarephath with Elisha's predecessor who in the time of spiritual famine only had a little meal (the Word of God) and a little oil (the anointing)! But unlike the Widow of Zarephath, whose task was to support the prophet until the appointed time, this woman's task was to exercise what she still possessed in God.

Bring in all the vessels you can find, borrow from anyone you can, and bring them into the House of God so that they may be filled with oil. Do you believe God? Do you REALLY believe? Then bring in the vessels, not a few. Bring in the souls to the House of God so they may be filled. Do you believe in Salvation? Do you believe in Hell? The extent of your vision is determined by the depth of your faith. And when your faith is done, then close the door.

Faith allows God to multiply the anointing. He will not pour out His Spirit on a church that does not believe Him. But when faith grows, so will the outpouring.

Is this the formula for revival? I believe so. While I am loud in proclaiming that no revival comes without repentance and that all revivals have to be prayed in with a desperation that drives us past the limitations of our own flesh, I am adamant that revival is first, foremost, and always about winning the lost. It is the primary principle to understanding revival. In the Book of Joel, God cries out to us to be ashamed because the harvest of the field is perished (Joel 1:11) and that He has cut off the corn, the wine, and the oil from the House of God as a result. When we turn our focus away from the burden of winning lost souls, we turn off the faucet to the Spirit of God.

The solution to seeing the anointing flow once more in the Church is to fix the problem that caused it to cease. Cry out to God, not for your personal blessings and prosperity, but for God to shower us with His Holy Ghost conviction. Dear God, allow us to see, allow us to repent, allow us to return. Have mercy on us so that we may, in turn, have mercy on others. Our children are sold to be bondmen to the world because they see no power in the Church. The anointing we once had when our husband was alive in the church has dissipated into a fading memory. We have a form of godliness, but we have denied the power thereof. We have a House, but it is nothing but a shell of the glory that it once had.

> *Therefore also now, saith the LORD, turn ye even to me with all your heart, and with fasting, and with weeping, and with mourning: And rend your heart, and not your garments, and turn unto the LORD your God: for he is gracious and merciful, slow to anger, and of great kindness, and repenteth him of the evil.*
>
> *Who knoweth if he will return and repent, and leave a blessing behind him; even a meat offering and a drink offering unto the LORD your God?*
>
> (Joel 2:12-14)

About the Author

Dalen Garris has been in ministry since the Jesus Movement in California in 1970. In 1997, he began a radio broadcast that ultimately spread to dozens of countries, from Israel and Saudi Arabia to Africa and the Philippines. His program, *Fire in the Hole*, was broadcast for several years across North America on the Sky Angel network as the Voice of Jerusalem.

A newspaper column followed, which has been published in local newspapers and Christian magazines in several countries. He has also written over a dozen books and several booklets.

Since 2004, he has been lighting the fires of revival in churches spread across sub-Saharan Africa. Over the course of 17 years, he has preached in over 1,200 churches and has seen hundreds of them set on fire and explode with growth and hundreds of new ones planted across Africa. Hundreds of people have been supernaturally healed during the healing lines that so often sprang up during these revival meetings, and tens of thousands have been saved.

And the fires are still burning.

Because of his work across Africa, Dalen Garris was awarded an honorary Doctorate in 2017 by the Northwestern Christian University of Florida.

Dr. Garris currently lives with Cindy, his wife of 44 years, in Waxahachie and is still heavily involved with churches across Africa. His pressing hope is to see this powerful move of God in Africa ignite us here in America. He believes that this upcoming generation will be the Gideon Generation that will usher in this last, great revival that he has preached about for so many years.

If you would like Dr. Garris to speak at your church or organization, please contact us for times and schedules.

Books by Dalen Garris:

Available at: www.Revivalfre.org/books

- Four Steps to Revival
- Do You Have Eternal Security?
- Standing in the Gap
- Two Covenants
- Fire in the Hole

Revival Campaigns
- The Kenya Diaries
- A Trumpet in Nigeria
- A Scent of Rain
- Into the Heart of Darkness
- Fire and Rain
- Revival Campaigns in Africa – 2019
- The Battle for Nigeria
- A Light in the Bush
- A Match in Dry Grass
- Planting a Seed in Liberia
- A Whisper in the Wind
- Talking With the Women, by Cindy

A Voice in the Wilderness series:
vol. 1, The Journey Begins
vol. 2, the Early Years
vol. 3, Prophet Rising
vol. 4, Revival in the Wings
vol. 5, Sound of an Abundance of Rain
vol. 6, Watchman, What of the Night?
vol. 7, Mud and Heroes
vol. 8, Ashes in the Morning
vol. 9, Shaking the Olive Tree
vol. 10, Winds of Change
vol. 11, A Final Call
vol. 12, Superficial Shells

Booklets

Available at: www.Revivalfire.org/booklets/
A Volcano in Cape Verde
Tanzania, 2011
Nigeria, 2012
Calvinism Critique

RevivalFire Ministries

PO Box 822, Waxahachie, TX 75168

dale@revivalfire.org

www.Revivalfire.org

www.ingramcontent.com/pod-product-compliance
Lightning Source LLC
Chambersburg PA
CBHW060833050426
42453CB00008B/682